Getting Projects Done

by Michael S. Dobson, PMP

SideWise Publishers

Dedication

Once again, to my beautiful, brilliant,
and wonderful wife of 35 years

Deborah Singer Dobson

Table of Contents

List of Tables and Figures

Introduction

THE PROJECT MANAGEMENT INSTITUTE'S OFFICIAL definition of "project" has two essential characteristics: *temporary* and *unique*. Projects end, and while projects may be similar, they're never exactly the same. If you have what people call an "ongoing project," you have a problem. Either what you're doing is not really a project, or it is a project, but in bad trouble. Some projects get stuck at the 90 percent complete point and tend to stay there, which costs energy and focus and doesn't get results. Finish your projects or kill them: there is no middle ground.

Projects are unique in at least some essential elements, even when they're structurally similar. For example, you might be responsible for organizing your company's participation in several trade shows. Each trade show is a project—it ends. And even though each trade show has numerous elements in common with every other trade show, each will also have unique elements.

Because projects are temporary and unique, many of the normal standards and disciplines of the world of work don't quite apply. Often, there's a lot at stake, so the interest of top management may be much higher, and their involvement more active. Because there are no cookie cutter projects, it may well be that neither you nor anyone else in your organization fully understands what you're up against. Deadlines may be arbitrary, and even arguably unfair.

Project management is a discipline that was invented in the trenches. Almost all the techniques and tools—from the Gantt chart to critical path theory—were originally invented by active project managers trying to cope with the special circumstances of their own project. Some techniques turn out to be applicable and useful in a wide range of project circumstances, and they've been tested under battlefield conditions over many years.

Your projects are unique. But practicing project managers in many different situations experience similar problems and similar challenges and have risen to meet them. And when you master the practical tools and concepts of project management, you'll find that your ability to get your projects done the right way—on time, on budget, to the agreed-upon standard—is remarkably improved.

Chapter 1:
Kick-Starting Project Management

ALL TOO OFTEN, NEW PROJECT MANAGERS THINK THE first step in project management is to acquire the right software. Instead, you need the right mindset, the right attitude, the right wisdom. When your software tells you you're behind schedule, the project management question is, "What can we do about it?" Your ultimate goal is to get the project done on time, within the budget, and to a satisfactory level of performance. Tools may give you insight and help identify places where action is possible, but tools alone are not project management. If you don't get the job done, nobody cares why. And if you *do* get the job done, nobody cares why either.

Your attitude and your understanding are the most important tools you possess.

It's Not Just a Job, It's an Attitude

Project managers are people who think like project managers.

A project is a temporary activity, often started without full understanding of what the project will eventually entail, containing an inherent level of risk and uncertainty, and normally taking place alongside other work. What if you are the kind of person who is uncomfortable without a routine? What if you get more interested in the work process than in the goal? What if you don't completely agree with the people who are giving you the project assignment? The wrong answers to any of these questions can leave you at a significant disadvantage when it comes to managing your way through the project.

Your attitude, mindset, and picture of what's going on have a substantial impact on you, the members of your team, your customers, and those higher up in your organization. If you are confident, others around you will tend to be more confident. If you panic, don't be surprised when others around you fall into despair.

The Perfect Project Manager

Project management is a hybrid occupation. One aspect of project management is technical: command of certain analytical tools that enable you to structure and analyze your project. The other aspect is human: the ability to manage people in a highly fluid and uncertain environment. Both are important to your success..

How do we determine what the perfect project manager would look like? One way is to look at those who are already successful. Outstanding project managers have many of the following characteristics:

Technical. The perfect project manager has strong competence in technical matters as well as a commitment to personal self-development. Technical competence involves both those areas relevant to the subject matter of the project as well as project management in general.

- **The perfect project manager is analytical.** One of the most powerful tools available to the project manager is analysis: the process of breaking down a project into its components, determining the characteristics of those components, and using the knowledge and insight to create a solid plan.

- **The perfect project manager is process oriented.** The Project Management Institute (PMI®) says that project management can best be described in terms of component processes, methods by which a project—any project—can be broken down and organized. The more unfamiliar you are with the project you're managing, the more complex it is, or the more important it is, the more you will find attention to process helpful in getting your mind wrapped around it.

- **The perfect project manager knows the tools.** Much of this book will set forth the detailed tools specific to project management. Technical competence in these tools is important, but not sufficient. You have to understand why each tool is valuable, what it gives you as a project manager, and how to balance the work required to use the tool with the benefit you can receive.

- **The perfect project manager knows the subject**. Projects involve specific subject areas, and your technical understanding of the relevant subject areas is clearly important. Having said this, it is not unusual for a project manager to be assigned a project with major elements outside his or her subject expertise. When you're not knowledgeable, you need to develop good sources of information, interview experts, and pay special attention to the details so you can get the project done correctly.

- **The perfect project manager knows the system.** Projects take place inside organizations, and organizations have their unique dynamics. Your understanding of your own organization, industry, and environment is a crucial underpinning of your success.

Human. No matter how technically complex or sophisticated the project, project managers generally agree that it's the people and the politics that take most of your time and energy. Because project managers often are promoted from the technical ranks, they often find that they must work hard to supplement their technical skill base with improved skills on the people side. Core competencies include these factors:

- **The perfect project manager understands people.** Human behavior is motivated behavior, and as a project manager you need to know why people are behaving the way they are, especially if you hope to achieve change in that behavior.
- **The perfect project manager understands politics.** Politics, in a fundamental sense, is the unofficial way the organization makes decisions and allocates resources. It is a forum in which people

exercise different types of power in order to achieve their goals. You ignore the political realities of your organization at your own peril. As a project manager, remember that you have limited direct authority to achieve your goals—the unofficial methods of gaining and using power are central to your success.

- **The perfect project manager understands sales and negotiation.** Are you a professional salesperson or negotiator? Before you answer "no," think again. Do you have to sell your ideas, your vision, and your needs to an unsympathetic audience? Do you have to negotiate with others to get the resources, time, and tools you need to accomplish your projects? If you find that you are cast in the role of a salesperson or negotiator, then it's clearly a good idea to master the skills that the professionals use.

- **The perfect project manager radiates confidence.** It's easy to be a manager on a good day. It's a lot tougher when everything seems to be falling apart all around you. That's when you discover that part of leadership is acting. The ability to look calm and confident when others around you are losing their heads is a powerful influencer. People look to the project manager for hope, for cues, and clues of what behavior is appropriate. When you aren't confident, learn to project it anyway. That isn't lying, because when others also become calmer and more confident, the chance of success goes up tremendously.

- **The perfect project manager works hard.** You'll frequently hear the time management slogan, "Work smart, not hard." It's clearly true that work that isn't smart often isn't relevant, and working hard on things that are useless and unproductive doesn't achieve a good outcome. But to conclude that hard work isn't part of the equation is rather naïve. The project manager normally needs to work smart *and* hard, not only to get the job done, but also to serve as a role model for others to emulate.

- **The perfect manager keeps the goal in mind.** It is hard to stay focused on a long-term goal in the face of short-term catastrophe. Nevertheless, that's the challenge set before you.

Exhaustive? Not at all. But it's a good start to understanding the core competencies of project managers. To be a first-rate project manager, you need to be a first-rate manager—and even a first-rate human being. It's a lifelong challenge, and nobody does it perfectly. Set these as overall goals, and feel good about yourself when you make progress.

Why Better is Better (And Why Sometimes Good Enough Really Is)

It's easy to optimize a system to achieve a single goal, but often it's the wrong thing to do. Project managers are very familiar with the need for tradeoffs. That's why another of the attitudes of the effective project manager is not making perfect the enemy of good. Our project is seldom the only project going on.If making our project great does enough damage to other projects, it may not be the best choice from the company's perspective.

In an imperfect world, we must often work with incremental improvements. "Better is better" is a project manager's attitude, even if the outcome is less than ideal.

If our project outcome cannot be perfect, then how good must it be? In other words, exactly how good is good enough? This is often a crucial question for the project manager.

Start each project by identifying what would be the ideal outcome, and then what would be an acceptable, or good enough outcome. To do this, remember that a project is a means to an end, rather than an end in itself. Focus on the goal to be achieved, and work backwards to find the satisfactory achievement level. We'll go into this method in more detail later.

The Godzilla Principle

Project management is also often about risk management, and there's a general rule of problem solving known as the Godzilla Principle.

In the archetypal Japanese monster movie, there's usually a scene early on where the monster *du jour* is small and helpless. One prescient actor urges everyone to kill the baby monster, but no one else agrees. Later, usually after exposure to radiation or some exotic pollutant, the monster grows to giant size and begins to destroy Tokyo. Now, of course, everyone in the street is yelling, "What are we going to do?"

Fig 1. The Godzilla Principle

Project managers know the answer, and the answer is obviously to kill the monster while it's still in embryo. Another of the important elements in project management is the art of early detection and management of project risks. As a general rule, if you catch it early, it's easier to kill. That's the Godzilla Principle in project management.

The project management approach is to put more time into the initial phases of the project: determining what the project is and what approach will be taken (project initiation), and analyzing the project carefully to create a set of plans (project planning). These steps will almost invariably reduce the amount of firefighting and reactive behavior on the project. Do it right the first time (plan in advance) and then you won't have to find the time to do it over.

Some Barriers Are Illusory

In any project, it's normal that we have real problems, real barriers, real obstacles, real limitations that prevent us going in certain directions. It's often the case, however, that at least some of what we perceive to be unbreakable obstacles are not what they seem. As you learn project management tools and concepts, you'll often discover that some barriers are illusory, that you often have more time, more money, and more flexibility than you thought at first, that there are options available that previously you couldn't even see.

Attitude and perspective are powerful tools, and they don't depend on outside circumstances. You'll discover that as you adopt a philosophy of hope, others will find it easier to follow you. They will likely work harder and show greater creativity than might otherwise be the case. And when you approach the problems and barriers with a can do attitude, you'll discover that some of them diminish considerably.

Project Management Makes the Critical Difference

Most of the project management tools and concepts we use today were originally developed in response to real-world operational problems. Unlike some currently popular management ideas, they were not conceived academically, although they have subsequently been explored and formalized in an academic context.

Above all, project management is an increasingly popular toolset because it *works*. By following the reality-tested processes and using the analytical tools, you come to a deeper understanding of the nature of your project, the potential pitfalls, the hidden resources, the constraints and challenges, and the creative opportunities that empower you to get the job done.

Project management can make the critical difference for you and your organization in facing the complex and difficult challenges ahead.

Projects within Projects

Again, projects are temporary and unique: without an intent to finish, there is no project. There are some special cases, though. Let's look, for example, at a new product launch. What exactly is the project? It includes a marketing campaign, of course, but for the product to launch, you have to have a product. The product must be manufactured, but before it can be manufactured, it must be designed. Perhaps it must be tested, or undergo regulatory approval as well. Before you know it, you end up with something like this:

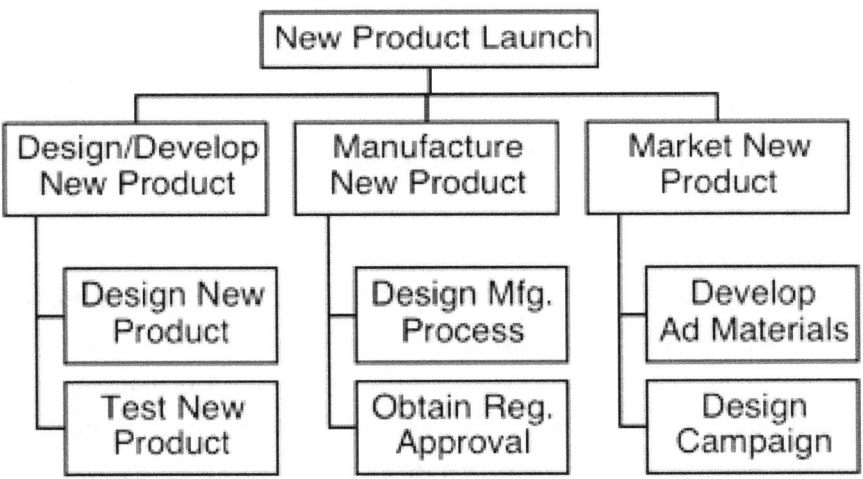

Fig 2. Single Project or Collection of Projects?

If you're in charge of the overall new product development project, your responsibility is the top box on the chart, and all subordinate boxes are only project phases or project elements. But if you're in charge of one of the subordinate activities, such as designing the marketing campaign, that's a perfectly legitimate project as far as you're concerned. So to some extent, the answer to the question "What is a project?" depends on your perspective. Where you stand depends on where you sit.

It's important to know if your project is part of an *über*-project, because it influences your understanding of the right way to go about it. Your individual choices as a project manager are constrained by the higher project. Your deadline and budget may be determined in reference to the higher project. How good is good enough is also determined by the higher project.

Projects and Operations

The world of work is made up of *projects* and *operations*. Projects, as we've seen, are temporary and unique. They have a purpose and once the purpose is achieved, the project goes away.

Operations, by contrast, are ongoing. There is no planned or intended point when we plan to stop. Managing the accounting department is operational work: there will be an accounting department as long as there is a company. Closing the books at the end of the fiscal year, however, can be considered a project. It has an intended finish, even if you're going to do it again next year.

Even if your environment is primarily operational, projects often creep in. By the very nature of a project, work tends to be disrupted. Additional resources must be deployed. One of the challenges you have as a project manager is that the operational work normally still has to get done even while the project is going forward — and it's not unusual that the same people have responsibility for both. The balance of work vs. project must be carefully monitored and maintained.

Balancing Priorities among Multiple Projects

Not only is it challenging to manage a project when most resources must be devoted to operations, but it is also challenging to manage a project when other projects compete for the same resource pool. We might not be doing a single new product for release this year, but perhaps six or seven new products. Each requires design, each requires test, each requires manufacturing, each requires approvals, each requires a marketing campaign, and so forth.

Even if the subject matter is the same, the value of the projects usually isn't. Some products are more difficult or expensive to develop; some products have greater or lesser sales potential. Some products have champions or draw the attention of people at high levels. You've got to be realistic about where your project fits into the big picture. Sometimes you have the right of way; other times you must yield to more valuable or important projects, even if your project suffers in the process.

Throwing It Over the Wall

In a traditional organization in which specialists are grouped together (engineering, marketing, accounting, information technology), you can easily have a situation in which projects move "sideways" through the organization, worked on by specialists in individual departments before being transferred to the next stage.

Accountability is difficult in this situation. If you are the project manager for the entire project, you normally have a home in one of the departments; say, engineering or marketing. It would be highly unusual if you were expert in each of the numerous disciplines needed to get the project out. You must rely on people in the different departments to apply their special knowledge and skills. You're unlikely to be the direct supervisor of all the people you need; possibly, some of the technical experts and specialists are higher in rank than you.

Technical experts have a tendency to elevate their own discipline and skill over others, and so each wants his or her piece to be as good as possible. Unfortunately, as we've seen, optimizing a project around a single good can create problems, so your project may find itself whipsawed among different specialties, each trying to maximize itself at the cost of others.

You vs. Other Projects

Now, even if everyone in the organization is committed to excellence and wants a great product to come out, notice that conflict is still inevitable because your product isn't the only one making its way through the system. Putting more effort or expense into Product A means that there is less available for Products B, C, and D.

When your organization is managing multiple projects, the balancing act gets even more complex. You must not only balance projects vs. work, one technical area vs. another, but now projects vs. other projects.

The most important step in bringing this process under control is to make priorities clear. That's relatively easy when the value of projects is clear. The trouble is that the reasons one project trumps another are often ambiguous and sometimes political.

Perhaps one of the products was the pet idea of one of the senior vice-presidents. On a more positive note, perhaps a product with little first-year sales potential is seen as critical to the organization's long-range strategy. Maybe the sales potential of two products is close enough that it's unclear which should properly take priority. In these cases, the balancing act is increasingly delicate.

If people with the requisite authority or organizational position don't see the conflict clearly enough (and if they aren't experienced in the discipline of project management, they may not), then you find yourself in an environment of shifting priorities, which complicates any attempt at project scheduling.

If you are working in a multiple project environment, even if you're not the overall portfolio manager, try to put together a list of all projects competing for the same resources. For each project, look for the factors that should elevate it or lower it in relative priority. Show your list to people in authority for modifications. If your project isn't on top of the list, make sure your plans and processes account for the likelihood that higher-priority projects will take extra resources, which will tend to delay or degrade your project.

Hidden Opportunities

What you often want and need is more time, more money and resources, and more flexibility in acceptable results. Fortunately, project management tools will uncover some hidden opportunities in virtually any project, and that is one of the most important benefits available to you as you master these skills.

For example, the bleak picture of inter-project conflict we just discussed can be turned around into an opportunity, if you look at it the right way. If your project is of lesser priority, then there are only three directions in which you can go: you can extend the deadline if the resources you need must be assigned elsewhere, you can obtain more resources (overtime, temporary help, second choice team members) if you can't extend the deadline, or you can lower the performance target of the project from excellent to good enough. Knowing how and when to exploit the flexibility in your project is an important skill.

Think you can't do any of these? Sometimes it seems as if your choices are constrained to the point of impossibility. However, since you can't do the impossible, something in your project is going to have to give. You're better off choosing than having fate choose for you, because the damage that will result is different depending on which way you go. Notice that if your project is of lower priority, senior management has already accepted the reality that damage to your project is more acceptable than damage to another, higher-priority one. So you need to determine which type of damage is most acceptable— or, alternately, least unacceptable.

By taking a close and careful look at the project's goal —the "Why?" behind the project—you can determine what to do. Why was the particular deadline chosen? Is it because of a fixed date, such as a trade show, or is it more general, such as out in time for the back-to-school market? Or was the deadline simply picked because someone needed a date and that one looked reasonable? If you miss launching your new product at the trade show, it may result in a substantial competitive disadvantage. But if the date was fairly arbitrary, less harm will result if you miss it.

Project Management as a Set of Processes

Project management can be understood as a set of component processes. According to PMI, there are five process groups: Initiating, Planning, Executing, Monitoring and Controlling, and Closing.

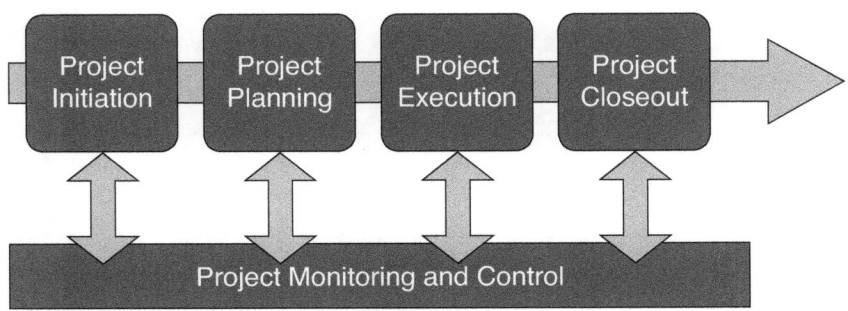

Fig 3. The Five Project Management Processes

The most important lesson to derive from the five processes is that there is a flow to project management. By doing each process well in turn, you go into subsequent processes with much greater control and with a lowered risk. If an early process is performed poorly or incorrectly, the damage may not become apparent until much later in the project, but the damage is done.

People without a background in project management have a tendency to get over-eager in the beginning phases, and rush through them so they can jump right into the execution of the project. From an outside perspective, that might look efficient, but it tends to generate a lot more late-project problems and even failures.

Do it right the first time according to the processes, and you'll find yourself in better shape at the end.

Chapter 2:
Initiating Your Project

A PROJECT IS NOT AN END IN ITSELF, BUT A MEANS TO an end. There are numerous steps, actions, and decisions that get performed before the project becomes official. This is known as the *Initiating* process group. It ends with the approval of the *Project Charter* (though it may be called something else in your organization), constituting official recognition of the project and the authority for the project manager to proceed.

Projects often go through numerous hurdles on the way, and quite a few don't even get off the ground. That isn't necessarily a bad thing — in fact, sometimes it's absolutely the right thing to do.

Birth of a Project

Project managers often find that before they can get on with the business of managing the project, they must be a project consultant first.

As we've mentioned, a project is not an end in itself, but a means to an end. If the project is to build a website, the first question that should concern you is "Why?" Why do we want a website? What problem will it solve? What opportunity are we attempting to exploit? Each possible answer results in a different approach to the project, and often generates questions of its own.

"We want to sell our product over the Internet." Okay, that's an answer, but it invites a follow-up "Why?" Why over the Internet? Why not through a catalog, or a store, or possibly over someone else's website?

The purpose of this exercise is not to say that we shouldn't have a website or sell our product over the Web, but rather to help discover the hidden assumptions and agendas your customer may have.

Sometimes the reason given reveals the lack of thought behind the project. "We want to sell on the Internet because everyone else is!" "Because everyone else is" is a reason to investigate further, but not sufficient reason to make a commitment to e-commerce. Perhaps the right next step would be a project to do a study and make detailed recommendations.

There can be more thoughtful reasons underlying a project as well. "We are looking to reduce the turnaround time of reorders for our installed customer base by using the Internet." The goal of reducing turnaround time gives you the first clues about the shape and nature of the site, and the criteria you can use to determine success or failure.

Compare this reason with the following: "We want to be able to offer our less-popular backlist items to customers but the cost of printing and mailing catalogs is too high for the potential volume of business. By using the Internet, we would like to have a low-cost way of offering a large number of items to our customers."

Would you produce the same website for these two customers? Almost certainly not. In the first case, a critical quality factor is speed; in the second case, the issue is cost. How, then, can you produce any website for a customer without a good understanding of the actual business problem or opportunity?

Don't automatically expect your customer to supply this for you. Your customer, whether external or internal, may not have thought the problem through at a conscious level, or may not possess the expertise or insight to ask for the right things. It's a mark of the outstanding project manager that we meet needs that the customer isn't necessarily able to articulate!

Framing the Project

It's often the case that at least some of this process has been done in discussions that led up to the decision to do a project in the first place. But it's not necessarily the case that you receive the complete story when the project lands in your lap.

The Process of Starting a Project

A well-run business operates from a long-term strategic plan, which is ideally encapsulated in the form of a mission or vision statement. Based on the strategic plan and the current business environment, the executive leadership determines objectives for a fiscal year or quarter or other measurement period. At a departmental level, a variety of problems, opportunities, and threats are considered to see which ones would be most beneficial to attack, and from there come projects. The projects, to be effective, have to relate back up the chain to support the goals and objectives of the organizations.

With all of this, what is often overlooked is that the operational project manager who is responsible for the project is not necessarily a member of the senior leadership team, and isn't privy to all the discussions and work that went into establishing the project in the first place. Without an understanding of the context of the project, you find yourself shooting in the dark, with the likelihood that you won't hit the target the organization needs you to hit.

Trace each project back to the goal or purpose it serves, because only with that knowledge can you begin to make smart decisions.

The Project Manager Arrives

If there hasn't been a decision to start a project, obviously, there's no need to have a project manager. Much of the pre-project phase is done without a formal assignment of a project manager. The disadvantage is that some options you might otherwise have had are foreclosed by the process.

The most dangerous word that ever came out of a project manager's mouth is, "Yes, I'll do it," if said before you have a full understanding of what it is you're being asked to do.

Start with a positive attitude, of course, but understand that your initial objective is to find out the

full story. And that means asking—and listening to—
what people are requesting, even if you believe their ideas
are wrong-headed and even self-destructive. The first goal
of the project manager is to understand what is being
asked of you. Then—and only then—are you in a position
to give informed consent to the proposed project.

Here is a list of questions to consider when discovering
what your project is really about. Make sure in asking the
questions that you don't come across as trying to give
someone the third degree. The purpose of these questions
is discovery, not challenge. You need to know what people
are thinking, whether or not you end up agreeing with
their thought processes.

- When the project is successfully completed, what
  will be different for the organization?
- Who helped in the decision to choose this project?
- What specific deliverables must be produced for
  this project?
- What resources will be available for this project?
- What other demands will be placed on those
  resources?
- Where does this project fit with other priorities of
  the organization?
- Who will decide how to measure whether the
  project succeeds or fails?
- How will we measure success or failure?
- Why was the specific deadline chosen?

- What other options or choices were considered in choosing this project?

Based on the answers you get, you may be ready to give a cheerful "Yes!" to the project, you may want to work at helping people understand why the project is a bad idea, or you may need to do some negotiation to end up with a workable project objective.

Negotiating the Objective

Often, project managers feel at an organizational disadvantage. As a general rule, the people who assign projects tend to outrank those who manage or perform projects. When you're given a direct order, you're pretty much stuck—aren't you?

Usually, not as much as many project managers suppose. After all, you share one goal with those who assign the projects: you want it done. If it can't be done under the circumstances, do you really please your superiors by going ahead and failing? In most cases, the blame for failure ends up on your shoulders even if you knew from the beginning that the project was going to crash and burn.

That's justified, up to a point. After all, once you accept a project, even if you felt coerced, it is yours, for better or worse. The failure of the project doesn't meet the objectives of those who assigned the project to you. Therefore, both you *and they* end up better off if you negotiate a workable project objective in advance.

Negotiating from a weak organizational position. From a power down position in the hierarchy, it often appears that negotiation is out of the question, but that's often not true. In our discussion of the perfect project manager, we listed negotiation skill as one of the core competencies, and you need to use that skill from the beginning of the project all the way through. You do this not merely for your own self-protection (though of course that's perfectly legitimate), but also for the good of your customers, your superiors, and the organization. It benefits no one if the project fails, especially if you've now spent all the money, resources, and time.

The three steps of negotiating project objectives. There are three basic steps to follow in negotiating project objectives.

- The *first step* is to make it clear that your goal is to achieve *their* goal, that you are planning to do your very best to ensure the project succeeds. Your purpose in negotiating an objective isn't to make your life easier (though if that's an incidental benefit, so much the better), but to develop the most realistic objective in support of the most productive and worthwhile goal.

- The *second step* is to understand (from your questioning) what is negotiable and what is not.

- The *third step* is to keep yourself (and those with whom you are negotiating) focused on the shared goals: a successful project, a successful organization. The negotiation becomes about methods and options. When it moves onto this principled level, you become stronger in the negotiation, because it isn't any longer simply about rank, but about the best way to get the job done.

Timing. Do remember that your power to negotiate is greater before the project has officially begun than it will be later on. Withhold the "Yes!" and focus on the "How?" and "Why?" in your initial work on the project.

The Big Picture (and the Hidden Agenda)

The big picture. Projects take place inside an overall context. If your project is to develop a website to sell product on the Internet, it makes a difference if some competing company has just started offering online reordering. The urgency of the project has increased, for one thing, and the definition of quality now includes benchmarking.

Benchmarking is a technique for identifying and measuring quality goals against an established reference point. Using benchmarking allows you to compare conditions, processes, or results, and to identify potential improvements and quality goals, i.e., exactly how good is good enough. If your goal is to be the best in your field, and you can figure out what is currently the best, you can establish that as a benchmark. If you're at least that good, you're tied for first place; if you're better, then you're the best. Of course, if the other side is smart, they'll be benchmarking against you.

It's difficult to achieve agreement on measurement points for your project, especially when you're working with customers with limited knowledge of your field. By establishing a benchmarking effort, you have the power to set an objective standard, eliminating ambiguity and confusion about whether you've hit the target.

The hidden agenda. Another prime danger in the initial phase of your project is the existence of a hidden agenda behind the project request. People want projects because of their results, of course, but there may be additional factors, such as competition or rivalry among managers, a personal stake in the outcome, a battle for possession of organizational turf, or more. Because the hidden agenda is a customer need or desire, you need to know about any hidden agendas up front. If you fail to satisfy a hidden agenda, you may end up with a customer displeased at your project result, whether or not you did what you were told to do.

Fortunately, most hidden agendas are not hidden very deeply, and with a little attention to this critical area, you should be able to uncover most of them.

Uncovering Hidden Agendas

Start by assuming that one or more hidden agendas are operating. They may be quite benign—many people get personal benefit from doing what's right for the organization, and knowing that the company will make a profit *and* your boss gives you a second reason to succeed.

Look for ways the requester benefits. Most projects are done for organizations, but individuals request them. How does the individual who is requesting the project stand to benefit by the project's success? Is there a benefit the requestor may get if the project fails (e.g., the pleasure of saying "I told you so," or a concern that the project's success might involve eliminating some jobs)?

Look at the requestor's relationships. Does the requestor have friends or enemies in high places whose interests may be advanced or hampered by the project's success?

Look at the requestor's relationship with you. Does your success benefit or please the requestor, or would the requestor prefer to see you fail?

Ask around. Who do you know who has a relationship with the requestor, and whom you can ask for information?

Don't assume you have the final answer. Keep your eyes open and pay attention throughout the project, and if something happens that doesn't appear to make sense, assume that it might be an indicator of a different agenda, and do some hard analytical thinking about it.

Establishing the project objective involves careful attention to your customer. A lot of listening, a list of good questions (focusing on "Why?"), and benchmarking against existing targets is a critical part of getting ready to manage the project.   Finding out what people want doesn't automatically mean we're able to deliver. Our choices are constrained in a project environment, and next we'll look at those constraints, with emphasis on the Triple Constraints, one of the most powerful insights in all of project management.

The Triple Constraints

Everybody knows the old joke: "Did you want it good, fast, or cheap? Pick two." As with many management jokes, there's some truth buried under the humor.

At the heart of the Triple Constraints is a simple truism: because a project is temporary, there is a time constraint, which is the deadline. There is also a cost constraint (which includes dollars and resource expenditures), and a performance standard that you must meet. This is normally displayed as a graphic, thus:

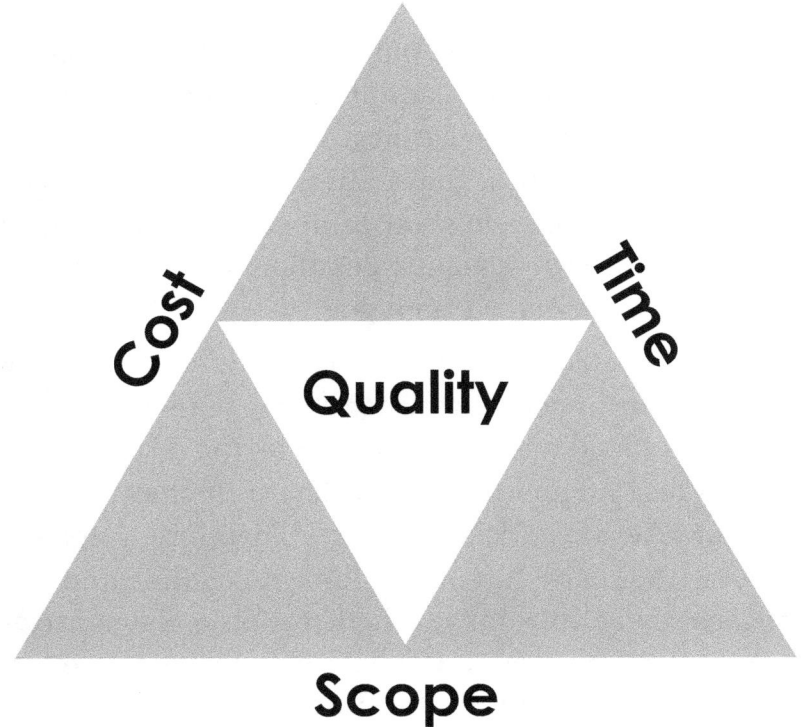

Fig 4. The Triple Constraints

The Universe of Every Project

What makes a project easier or harder to accomplish are the specific constraints imposed on it. A constraint is a restriction that limits the project team's options and affects performance, cost and/or scheduling. A project always has the Triple Constraints of time, cost, and performance, but may have additional constraints as well.

The constraints are often what make a project possible or impossible, and discovering and analyzing the constraints, therefore, is also one of the first steps in project management.

Time constraint. The time constraint may come in the form of an absolute deadline, or in a more general form, such as a plea for urgency. What makes a time constraint legitimate is that failing it has consequences. If you're designing a trade show exhibit, the opening day of the trade show is an absolute deadline. Fail to be ready, and the show goes on without you.

A time constraint can be absolute even if it's unknown. Let's say your project is getting the house ready for a new baby. The official due date provided by the doctor is, as we know, at best an approximation. The child may be born before or after the official due date. Therefore, you have a project with an absolute but unknown deadline and you'd better be ready. Normally, this turns into pressure to get the project done by the worst-case deadline, or to separate the project into essentials and optionals, and make sure the essentials are complete.

A statement like, "We'd like to have the project done in time for our annual meeting," represents a less-than-absolute time constraint. There may be some adverse consequences from failing to be ready in time for the annual meeting, but those consequences may be a lot less damaging than failing to meet the performance criteria or cost constraint.

Cost constraint. The cost constraint limits what you can expend to meet your project goal. One category of expenditures, obviously, is money, and a project normally has a budget, often with consequences for exceeding it. A person-hour is also an expenditure, and the cost constraint may be expressed not so much in terms of money, but in terms of human resource expenditures. You may have absolute limits on the number of person-hours available from a resource possessing unduplicated technical skills. Finally, a cost constraint can be defined in terms of other scarce resources.Like the time constraint, elements of the cost constraint can be absolute or more general. If the money, people, or materials just aren't available, then the constraint is absolute. If the organization would prefer you not spend too much money on the project, that's more general, and you may have some flexibility.

Scope. The third leg of the Triple Constraints consists of the essential performance criteria for the project, or what the project is supposed to do or have to be considered successful.You'll occasionally see someone define the Triple Constraints as consisting of time, cost, and quality.

This is a serious misunderstanding.

Scope is what the project *does* and quality is what the customer *wants*. Quality, and the satisfied customer that results, is certainly a goal of the project. In Figure 3, the points of the Quality triangle push against the Triple Constraint. The Triple Constraint is "good enough;" quality is the pressure to do more and better.

In the real world, however, we are frequently forced into tradeoffs—sometimes painful tradeoffs—among the Triple Constraints to get the project done, and that's why "good enough" is vital to know.

Misunderstandings about quality are also possible, and by developing a definition of performance criteria, you can check with the customer and confirm that this is the way to meet essential needs.

Remember that quality, for some customers, can represent factors more suited to the time constraint or the cost constraint.

Making the third leg of the Triple Constraints a definition of performance forces you to determine what is essential and what is optional; what is good enough and what is unsatisfactory.

Other constraints. The Triple Constraints hold true everywhere, but there can be many additional constraints on your project. If you're building a new factory, regulatory requirements such as building codes and zoning may limit your choices on the project. These requirements are constraints.

The state of today's technology can be a frustrating constraint. We might be able to accomplish it with ease five years from now, but right now, we can't get it to work with the tools we possess.

The macroeconomy can be a constraint. Are we in a recession? Has the business sector that employs us gone through a crash? Or are we in a period of such economic growth that we can't find enough skilled help because demand is so high?

The laws of physics can even be a constraint if you're sending up a spacecraft. So can the laws of governments if they prohibit or restrict certain actions in support of your project goals.

Don't forget *risk*. While risk is generally an environmental factor, how much risk you're able or willing to accept forms a constraint as well.

In an early meeting with your project team, try to develop a comprehensive list of constraints on your project. Test each to see how firm a constraint it actually is. For those that remain real constraints, know that you will have to build your project around their limitations.

Why Triple Constraints Analysis is Vital

If you don't know what your Triple Constraints are, you don't yet know enough to start on the project. Don't be surprised if your original project assignment was given to you in a form that left out one or more of them. People unfamiliar with project management may well not know the Triple Constraints.

If you don't get all three to begin with, another early-onset job you have as a project manager is to fill in the blanks, to determine any missing constraints and analyze their effect on your project.

While creativity and hard work will allow you to succeed on many projects in spite of constraints, you may run into a project where the constraints as defined make it clear that there is no possible way to complete the project. There may be consequences for calling this to the attention of your managers and customers, but compare that to the consequences of spending all the time and money and then failing.

If you can't get it done within the Triple Constraints, there are two possibilities: 1) don't do the project, or 2) get the constraints modified.

The Hierarchy of Constraints

On any project, the three legs of the Triple Constraints have different weights. Sometimes the time constraint is on top, sometimes the cost constraint, sometimes the performance criteria. Figuring out the right ranking for your project opens up a wide range of insights and even opportunities.

There are names for the hierarchy:

- **Driver**. The Driver of the project is the constraint that must be met at all costs, or else the project will be considered a failure.

- **Middle Constraint**. The second level of the Triple Constraints hierarchy, the Middle Constraint, has somewhat more flexibility than the Driver, but less than the Weak Constraint.

- **Weak Constraint**. This is the most flexible (but not necessarily the least important) member of the Hierarchy of Constraints. Exploiting the Weak Constraint is a powerful technique for helping to accomplish your project goals.

Exploiting the Weak Constraint

The first advantage of knowing the Weak Constraint is that it lowers pressure in at least one direction. If you find yourself in trouble on the project and cost is the Weak Constraint, you might decide that spending money and resources to get yourself out of trouble would be an alternative worth considering.

You can go further than that. You can deliberately exploit the Weak Constraint in order to improve your overall chances of project success. This isn't cheating; after all, the Weak Constraint is defined as having flexibility. Using that flexibility may be the smartest move you can make.

What can you do with the flexibility in *your* Weak Constraint?

The Triple Constraints concept gets a lot of space because it's crucial. It tells you what you have to accomplish, and it tells you where you have flexibility you can use. We'll find the Triple Constraints showing up again and again in our study of project management.

Of course, the Triple Constraints don't come out of thin air; they come from project stakeholders, who are customers and others with an interest in your project. Stakeholder management starts early and lasts throughout the project, so let's look at this important aspect of project management next.

Keep Your Friends Close, But Your Stakeholders Closer

A stakeholder is a person or an organization that is involved in or may be affected by project activities; someone with a vested interest in a specific outcome, or who exerts influence over a project.

What makes someone a stakeholder is their stake—the interest they have in the outcome (what you deliver) or the process (how it's done, what resources it consumes, how it affects other projects or activities) of your project.

Positive and Negative Stakeholders

The interest a stakeholder has in your project can be positive or negative from your point of view; that is, they may feel they benefit when your project succeeds, or they may feel they suffer a loss when your project succeeds. Since people often like to maximize their benefits and minimize their losses, you may expect positive stakeholders to support you and negative stakeholders to oppose you—but it can get a bit more complicated than that.

Positive stakeholders. Positive stakeholders feel they benefit by the success of your project, or at least have the potential to benefit from it. They can benefit because the product of your project is useful or profitable for them. They can benefit when the product of your project moves their goals further along. They can benefit when the work done on your project is reusable for their purposes.

Positive stakeholders are often in a position to benefit most if they can slightly modify the scope of your project so that their objectives fall into your area of responsibility, sort of like attaching an unrelated rider to a bill before Congress. In that sense, positive stakeholders can be a sort of potential conflict and trouble—one person's minor adjustment is another person's major headache.

Sometimes, the minor adjustments are indeed minor. If a small adjustment to your project can substantially increase the benefits from it, it may be very appropriate for you to accept the additional scope.

One way to increase the number of positive stakeholders on your project is to figure out ways slight modifications can expand the range of benefits to be obtained. Every person or organization that can benefit significantly is a source of support, extra funding in some instances, technical or political support, and much more. It's a win/win opportunity.

Negative stakeholders. Of course, some people or organizations may see your project as a net loss to them, either in the product or in the process of your project.

Here are some reasons people may be opposed to the product of your project. Perhaps your project will automate certain functions, allowing your company to lay off the people currently doing the work. Perhaps it may replace a comfortable, if old fashioned, system, with a modern high-tech one. Perhaps the success of your project will be an ego blow to someone who has been loudly arguing that it cannot possibly work.

People can also object to the process. Perhaps your project is taking resources that they need to achieve their own goals. Perhaps your project is disrupting their everyday work. Perhaps someone was hoping he or she would be assigned as project manager, and is unhappy that you have taken that role.

Negative stakeholders can be inside or outside the organization. Outside negative stakeholders can include business competitors, for whom your success means fewer customers for their offerings. There may be public interest or watchdog groups who believe your project is bad—it causes environmental damage, involves weapons technology, produces morally offensive entertainment, defames or damages a group of people, etc.—and should be stopped.

Regulatory and licensing organizations may be more neutral than negative, but their job is not to advance the success of your project, but to ensure that the interests they safeguard are protected. If you need FDA approval for your new drug, a UL seal for your new electrical product, or EPA clearance to build a chemical factory, you will need to recognize that their interests are not automatically in tune with your own, and work with them accordingly.

Managing Stakeholder Relationships

Make a written list of your stakeholders. Include name, organizational position, and the nature of their interest in your project. List whether the interest is positive or negative. Brainstorm ways you can gain better cooperation and support from positive stakeholders, and ways you can neutralize or turn around the interests of negative stakeholders. Consider doing this at home or someplace secure; you don't want an accidental copy of your notes to get around.

This strategy has two purposes. The first is that it's harder to be blindsided, but even better, it opens the opportunity for dialogue, and possibly changing an enemy into an ally—or at least into a neutral.

We don't mean to suggest that your project stakeholders are enemies (though it has been known to happen), but rather that actively managing stakeholder relationships from the very beginning of the project all the way through is another of the core success strategies in project management.

Working with negative stakeholders. Here's where the old adage "keep your friends close, keep your enemies closer" turns into practical advice. It's tempting to make an equation of negative stakeholder equals enemy, but that's not necessarily true at all. What makes someone a negative stakeholder is a different interest or goal. The first step, therefore, in working through any negative stakeholder situation is to identify who the person or organization is, and what their goal in the matter happens to be. You can understand their goal without necessarily sharing it. What you must keep clear in your mind is that their interest is real and legitimate to them.

Do everything in your power to open up a dialogue and build a relationship with your negative stakeholders.

First, you need to make absolutely sure you understand their goals. Paraphrase and double-check with them until they confirm your understanding.

Second, you need to see if there's any way you can satisfy those goals short of sabotaging your own project. (Of course, if you discover through the process of listening to your negative stakeholders that your project is in fact harmful and destructive, you may need to be in the business of stopping your own project. It doesn't happen often, but it does happen.) If an acceptable modification to your project eliminates their objections, you can turn some negative stakeholders into neutrals or even positive stakeholders.

Third, you need to keep an open line of communication and negotiation open even if a win/win resolution doesn't seem to be in the cards. By keeping them apprised of your project in an honest and straightforward way, you give them an incentive to play straight with you in return. If they then choose dishonorable tactics, you are in a better position to confront them or to let third-party observers know who is playing fair and who is not.

Fourth, remember that there's usually going to be more than one project. Peoples' positions and interests change, depending on what the project is. People who oppose you one day may be on your side the next, and if you have a reputation for trickiness and dishonesty, you may be buying yourself trouble on your next project.

How to Use Your Project Sponsor

It's normally the case that project managers aren't the most senior managers in the organization. The operational responsibility falls a little lower in the hierarchy than those who are responsible for programs (collections of projects, a general mission) and those who are responsible for departments. There are exceptions, of course, but this means that you normally don't have access to everyone you might need to work with. Therefore, you need to work on leverage with the higher-ups whose cooperation and support you often need to get the job done. The project sponsor is the manager in the performing organization who authorizes the project, allocates cash and other resources to perform it, and has executive responsibility for the project's successful completion.

You may or may not have a formal project sponsor identified by name, and sometimes this responsibility is parceled out among several managers (one provides cash, one controls certain key resources, one is in charge of the customer relationship), so you may have to do a little detective work to figure out who your key person is for the project.

You need the project sponsor because you need an ally of the appropriate management level to go where you can't go and make decisions outside your personal authority and scope. Operationally, the project sponsor is often the senior manager with the most active positive interest in having the project be a success. However, if that manager is not in your direct chain of command, you may find your access limited. Look in your own direct chain for the equivalent manager and work with that person as your project sponsor, but realize that it's sometimes the case that your own management chain of command is not very supportive of the project and can even be a negative stakeholder. (This is a very difficult position in which to find yourself, but do be aware that this situation can and does happen.)

Your project sponsor may have special interests of his or her own, and if you can accommodate those without destroying the project, it's often wise, because you need the help. Make sure to consider the situation from the sponsor's point of view.

Here are specific suggestions for working with your project sponsor:

- If your organization doesn't have a formal project sponsor role assigned, figure out who is doing the job.
- Decide where in your project your sponsor needs to be involved. Cut across functional lines for communication? Open doors? Arrange specific approvals?
- Not all project sponsors know they're project sponsors or what they are supposed to do. Talk to your sponsor and tell him or her the role you'd like them to play on the project.

- Ask your project sponsor what his or her definition of excellence and good enough are for the project. Don't assume you know without asking.

- Ask your sponsor what their own goals and objectives are for the project. Listen between the lines in case you're being tipped off to a hidden agenda.

- If heavy political pressure is being put on you by someone else, let your sponsor know about it and ask for help and advice—don't wait until after the fact.

- Figure out where your sponsor is in the formal hierarchy and in the political environment. If your sponsor is politically weak, you need to be aware of this up front. If your sponsor is extremely strong, you want to be careful you're always seen as an ally.

- If your project sponsor is not your immediate supervisor, make sure your immediate supervisor is kept up to date about the relationship so there's no opportunity for you to be seen as going behind someone's back.

- Ask for (and follow up on) a regular meeting with your project sponsor to talk about the project. Some sponsors want to be very much in the loop; others prefer sporadic briefings and a visit if there's trouble. Adjust the frequency of the meetings you request based on the sponsor's desires.

- Keep sponsor dealings confidential (except for the updates you provide your own supervisor), especially if they involve the sponsor's candid political assessments of other managers.

Most supervisors and sponsors hate to be surprised. Problems happen; that's understood. Do all that is in your power to provide advance warning when possible.

How to Use Other Stakeholders

Because stakeholders have interests and goals concerning your project, they often find it in their own best interest to assist and advise you. This can be an extremely powerful opportunity for you as a project manager.

Have up-front conversations with stakeholders as soon as you have identified them. Ask about their goals and objectives, and listen for clues to hidden agendas. As you prepare your plans, consider how stakeholders could be of support to the project, and specifically ask each stakeholder for the services you want. (You won't always get a "yes," but you'll frequently get at least some support.) Make sure that stakeholder needs for information are satisfied as much as possible without violating organizational confidences. On areas of particular interest to specific stakeholders, make sure they feel they have at least been asked for their input.

If you must do something that is contrary to the interests and goals of one or more of your stakeholders, tell them about it in advance unless telling them violates organizational confidences or policies.

Take care of your negative stakeholder relationships as thoroughly and professionally as you do your positive stakeholder relationships.

The Rules of Effective Influence

Influencing others and being organizationally effective is something that can repay a lifelong study. Here are some rules and principles you will find effective in gaining cooperation and support from your stakeholders:

- For short-term gain, *build common interests through negotiation.* For long-term gain, work on building trust, confidence, and mutual respect, and demonstrate your own integrity and honesty.

- Have the courage to *make necessary hard decisions,* and the empathy to work with people who may be negatively affected by those decisions.

- *Avoid making enemies.* An opponent merely wants something different; an enemy is personal. To keep opponents from turning into enemies, make sure you show integrity and honesty in all dealings, and don't be seen as a double-crosser or manipulator.

- *Be a worthwhile ally.* Be careful about offering your wholehearted and unreserved support, but do support people in their worthwhile goals even if there is no direct benefit to you. Don't be a fair-weather friend; demonstrate that you care about your allies even if there is some political risk to you. In the long run, you'll earn respect.

- Be generous and *do favors whenever possible.* In general, don't tie favors to specific quid pro quos; simply do favors when they are organizationally appropriate and within your power.

- *Ask for favors when you need help.* Don't remind people of previous favors; people of integrity will remember and act accordingly. If they are not people of integrity, you have learned something valuable about them.

- *Keep lines of communication open* across barriers and in times of conflict. Be open to diplomatic approaches and be prepared to negotiate on a principled foundation.

- Make it clear by your actions and choices that *you do what's right and beneficial to the organization.*

- *Show respect for the opinions and goals of those with whom you disagree.* Listen empathetically even if you cannot or will not adjust your position, and demonstrate that you understand contrary positions. Be willing to consider someone's arguments, even if you end up with the same decisions afterward.

- *Be aware that others do not necessarily follow the same code of principles that you do.* Act with integrity, but don't let yourself be blind to the reality of others' behavior.

- Remember that *no matter how important today's project may be, there is a tomorrow as well.* Unprincipled behavior may be a way to win a current fight, but other people notice and remember. A long term perspective pays off.

Stakeholder relationships show up in the Initiation phase of your project, but to manage your stakeholders properly you'll have to keep it up throughout the project life cycle. Relationship management is a crucial skill in almost any aspect of organizational life, and so it is here.

Stakeholders have different roles. We've discussed the customer as a stakeholder and the role of the project sponsor. As a project manager, you are obviously a stakeholder in your own project, and so are the members of your project team. Customer, sponsor, and team members are the core of your stakeholder community, and normally get your first and best support.

Negotiating a SMART Objective

The idea that the project objective is negotiable doesn't always jibe with the way you see your situation. Often, you may feel as if the decision has been made long before you come on the scene, and that it's another case of "yours not to reason why, yours but to do or die."

It's certainly true that there are limits to what can be negotiated. But look at it this way: if you ask the most overlooked question in project management—"Why?"—the answer you get reveals whether negotiation is possible.

There is a not-so-veiled threat in this negotiation approach, and that's just fine. Decisions have consequences, and helping people understand those consequences is one of the influence management techniques project managers have to use.

Does this mean that conflict is part of your duties as a project manager? Absolutely. Negotiation, even win/win negotiation, can involve some hardball from time to time.

Of course, if we're able to resolve the problem in a more collegial tone, so much the better. But conflict avoidance often doesn't work. If you don't push back against an unreasonable deadline or an impossible budget or unachievable performance at the beginning of your project, you'll likely fail, and then you'll have the same conflict—maybe worse—at the end of your project. It's tempting to avoid conflict if you can, but if all you're doing is postponing conflict, you've gained nothing.

Let's look at some common problems in negotiating objectives.

Resolving Conflicts in Multiple Objectives

Many times, conflict about objectives is unavoidable because you have multiple stakeholders. Each stakeholder wants his or her objectives as part of the project, but it may not be possible to satisfy all stakeholders. How do you resolve conflicts concerning multiple objectives?

Identify disparate objectives. The first part of the process is to identify all the objectives, whether or not you will be able to achieve them. Just as in our initial approach to a single-objective project, we must understand what is being asked of us separately from whether the goals are feasible. Wouldn't it be a shame to deal with scope creep, unhappy customers, or failure because you didn't ask early enough what people wanted? Sometimes it *is* possible to do what everyone wants.

Negotiate constraints. The second possibility is that you can do what everyone wants, but not within the constraints of time and/or cost. The good news is that you now have an opportunity to go back to your project sponsor or customer, explain the additional objectives and the value in achieving them, and try to get extra money and/or an extension to reach the revised goal. Again, sometimes this works quite well, and then you get it all done. And the worst they can say to you is "No."

Be willing to make hard choices. There are two scenarios left: 1) you can't get the extra time and money you need, and 2) some of the objectives people have are mutually exclusive. Either way, you can't do everything everybody wants, so someone's objectives won't be met. Negotiation is the only viable option.

In order, here are the steps to try to get an appropriate resolution to this kind of conflict:

- Get the affected parties together and let them negotiate with each other and let you know the decision. If they can't or won't, then...

- Rank the conflicting objectives by value to the customer or the performing organization, and select the highest value objective. If it isn't clear which has the highest value, then...

- Identify the political clout and willingness to use it among the stakeholders with the competing objectives, and do what the person with the most power to help you/harm you wants. If there's a tie, then...

- Look for people for whom one answer gives a benefit over another, and do what makes the greatest number happy. If it isn't clear, then...

- Give it to your supervisor, manager, or project sponsor, and ask him or her to choose. If that doesn't work, then...

- Prefer the faster to the slower, the easier to the harder, the simpler to the more complex. If there aren't significant differences, then...

- You might as well flip a coin.

Getting Specific

It's not unusual for an objective to start in a vague and general state, because not much is known or has been thought through at the very beginning. That's not a problem, as long as it doesn't stay in that state. Through questions and answers, through negotiation, and through a preliminary investigation, your job is to put a detailed structure onto the objective so you have a clear, workable target at which to shoot.

The famous acronym SMART is a good test to determine when you're finished. Is your objective...

Specific. An objective must have enough specific detail so you and your project team know what the final product or service is supposed to look like.

Measurable. Look for ways the project can be quantified. Objective standards (where possible) reduce the opportunity for conflict.

Reducing subjectivity in the process is to everyone's advantage. When the remaining subjectivity is limited in scope, negotiation and compromise can take you through to a satisfactory end. In the absence of any standards, both sides are deeply vulnerable.

Agreed to. Another important element in this process is that the standards of performance have been mutually negotiated and established before the project gets underway. If both sides have agreed on what they want in advance, there is less chance that the final product will turn out to be disappointing.

If the project involves numerous stakeholders, reaching agreement becomes more complicated, but also more important for the success of the project. By following the process for getting consensus on objectives, you are able to start the project with a clear statement of agreement about what is to be done.

Realistic. Negotiation is crucial if the initial request is not realistic. Sometimes a project has unavoidably high risk. The project may need to be modified (or sometimes cancelled), but if it has to go forward, everyone involved should be aware of the risks and consequences.

Look at exploiting flexibility and tradeoffs in the Triple Constraints. If the constraints are not subject to negotiation, we must live with them and their associated risk. If the constraints are negotiable, then the likelihood of success can often be improved.

Time constrained. There isn't always a deadline, but there's always a time constraint. Everything else being equal, getting a project done more quickly is almost always desirable for two reasons: 1) the benefit of the project is realized earlier, and 2) the resources the project takes are now free to take on new work.

Time can be a motivator. When there is no urgency, people tend to procrastinate. Imposing some time pressure on a project can be a useful supervisory tool for you to use as a team leader.

When your objective meets the SMART test, it tells you that you've got a statement clear enough to allow the work to take place.

Moving Towards Agreement

You can expect that the process of achieving a workable SMART objective will take more than one round, especially when multiple customers are involved. Don't worry if this take some time; you will likely save so much time in the rework that will otherwise be necessary that you'll come out ahead.

- Make sure you meet with all stakeholders in each round of the process. Stakeholders who feel left out and unable to make a contribution tend to put pressure elsewhere on your project. This is true even after a particular stakeholder's objective has been cut out of the project—protect their self-esteem and sense of participation.

- Summarize and paraphrase what each participant asks for in each round until he or she agrees that you understand. This is true even if your answer will end up being "No."

- As you complete a round, prepare a draft objective statement in writing, and give it to each stakeholder in turn as you begin the subsequent round. Invite feedback and discussion.

- You are finished when the objective is a) SMART and b) accepted by all stakeholders. A stakeholder whose objective has been cut doesn't have to like the final decision, but has to acknowledge that he or she understands that objective will not be in the final project.

Reality Testing

Sometimes it's clear that an objective is unrealistic from a simple inspection of the project. Other times, you cannot tell if a project is realistic until you're significantly into the work. This is particularly true in R&D projects or investigations where the act of doing the project is the only way to determine whether the project can be done.

If the project can't be done, it's not necessarily your fault. In R&D, finding out the answer *is* the project. If the answer is that you can't do it, that's an answer, even if it isn't a happy one. Learning to accept this type of failure as a kind of success is not something that comes easily and naturally. You may have to help members of your team past a sense of frustration or futility.

When you're working on a project like this, look for early ways to see if success is in the cards. The lower the level of sunk costs and sunk time in the project, the better off everyone will be.

If you must take on a high-risk project because of circumstances, then you will be bending all your energies toward finding a good answer, with no certainty that such an answer exists. You may find it desirable to take the public stand that "Failure is not an option," even though you won't be fooling anybody. That's motivation, and it can help. Your attitude as a leader will also shape the attitudes of your team. Putting in full commitment and top effort with the emotional position that victory is assured is the way to get the odds as much in your direction as they're going to get.

If failure results—and it can—then your next step is to ease the emotional burden of failure on yourself and others. The pain of failure can be just as great even if (at least intellectually) everyone knows that it was not the fault of the project team.

Understanding the Triple Constraints

If you've successfully created a written set of SMART objectives that your stakeholders have accepted, you're ready to move ahead to the next step. That step is to perform a Triple Constraints analysis as we did in the previous chapter. You may have used the Triple Constraints as a way to help build the SMART objective in the first place, but you should revisit them at this stage. They can change.

Objectives and Triple Constraints on a project should not change lightly or easily. If the objective mutates three times a day, that's a sign that you haven't really achieved agreement. But circumstances alter cases. Perhaps another project of higher priority has just been started, and your resources are taken away. Perhaps we learn that the competition is just about to release a new product that competes with yours, and your deadline has to be drastically moved forward. Perhaps you've gotten a new CEO, and organizational priorities change. When your macroenvironment changes, pull out your Triple Constraints and your hierarchy of Driver/Middle/Weak and look at them again. If your project has changed, you need to start modifying it as soon as practical.

Don't be surprised if you keep going two-steps-forward-one-step-back throughout the Initiation and Planning phases of your project. Each step in the process often reveals new facts and new problems that weren't apparent earlier. In fact, that's one of the big reasons to use the process.

We're also taking some important steps in customer relationship management by doing this work. The better the quality of your upfront agreement, the fewer challenges and obstacles you'll see later on.

Writing a Project Charter

The output of this phase of the project is a document known as a Project Charter. It's unimportant whether you call it a Project Charter or not, and the format can vary considerably. What is important is that you end up with a piece of paper (or occasionally papers) that sets forth the agreement to do the project and the desired destination. Without paper, you start your project in a state of vulnerability. As with most failures in the Initiation phase, the damage may not show up until much later.

Why a Project Charter Protects Both You and Your Project

Have you ever seen a project come into existence with no actual official decision to commit to it? This happens for many reasons: someone took a general verbal discussion to be an actual commitment, a project manager really wants to do this but management isn't sold on it, a senior manager wants to sink so much money into a particular project that it will be impossible later on for the organization not to finish it, or the organization simply has no formal process for project approval.

When this happens, everybody gets hurt. First, the leaders of the organization aren't aware of what commitments have actually been placed on staff members. New work gets added on, based on the official level of work already assigned, and because the other work isn't noticed, people get overburdened. When unofficial projects get into trouble, the lack of organizational commitment means that repairing the problems may be impossible. When projects are being run under the radar, a level of structural dishonesty permeates the organization, and trust vanishes.

When you use a Project Charter system, every project must have a charter before any expenditure of resources and money is authorized to. Projects have written goals and standards. There is clarity and focus in decision-making. The organization is in control of its work, and project managers are far less likely to be blindsided into impossible work.

What's in a Project Charter?

A Project Charter:

- Formally states the commitment of the organization to do the project.

- Provides a high-level summary of project objectives and goals.

- Assigns the project manager and states the authority the project manager has to make decisions and use resources in support of the project.

- Is issued (though not necessarily written) by the project sponsor.

There's a Project Charter template on the next two pages. By filling it out (a process that often requires some research), you'll have a good picture of what needs to be done. In addition to the items on the template, you might also consider the following.

Version control. Project charters may evolve during the process. For paper that may be modified, use version control numbers to ensure everyone's working with the most recent update.

PROJECT CHARTER TEMPLATE

GOAL	
PURPOSE OR JUSTIFICATION	
OBJECTIVES 1 2 3 4	**MEASURES OF SUCCESS** 1 2 3 4
IN SCOPE Done as part of the project.	**OUT OF SCOPE** Related to the project but done by others.
CONSTRAINTS Time Cost Scope ——— ——— ——— ———	**ASSUMPTIONS**

MAJOR RISKS	Likelihood and severity	ASSETS AND OPPORTUNITIES

STAKEHOLDERS	Concerns, importance, power	

MILESTONES/PHASES/KEY DATES		ASSIGNMENTS	
Milestone/Phase	Date	Customer	_____
		Sponsor/Manager	_____
		Project Manager	_____
		Team Member(s)	_____
			_____
		External Roles	_____
			_____
			_____

Fig 5. Project Charter Template

Decision. There must be a formal decision to do this project.

Triple Constraints. Information about the triple constraints is included, thought there may or may not be enough information included to determine the hierarchy of constrains. But the fundamental constraint is typically cited, along with the reason it is fundamental. For example, a product aimed for the Christmas season would have this as the time constraints.

Change control. Since scope creep is a danger on most projects, the Project Charter will typically forth specific and measurable design objectives that have been agreed to (that's S-M-A from our SMART acronym) for the project, and establish a change management process.

Priority and consequences. Since projects typically cut across functional department lines, there's always a predictable risk of conflict and lack of cooperation. The Project Charter should make it clear that a request for help isn't just from the project manager, but from the project sponsor.

Duties and responsibilities. The Project Charter will typically establish critical responsibilities and expectations for the project manager and for other departments or individuals who will need to cooperate. That's enough for a preliminary document like this. More detailed guidance will be in the plan.

Approvals. We discussed the role of the project sponsor in our discussion of stakeholders. The Project Charter should clearly identify the sponsor and make it clear that the sponsor plans to be a participant in the project and exercise certain control authority. Depending on the nature of your project, you may not find a complete match between this format and your situation. Different projects require different information. Other information that may be part of your Project Charter includes:

- A review of competitive projects
- Key stakeholders and their interests
- An historical description of the problem
- more detail about technical roles on the project and who will fulfill them
- Authorization to issue contracts
- Descriptions of other constraints and limitations.

Other Forms the Project Charter Can Take

If you are doing a project under contract for another organization, the contract itself may contain enough information to serve as the Project Charter. Preparing a repetitive document would be redundant. Sometimes other memos, reports, forms, or legal documents contain enough of the relevant information to serve the purpose. What's important about the Project Charter is the purpose, not the form.

In some organizations, the Project Charter can turn into something much more detailed and comprehensive, including a scope statement/statement of work, a Work Breakdown Structure (WBS) to at least the third level, a spending plan, resource requirements, résumés of key personnel, responsibility assignments, organizational structure, policies, and more. When done to that level, the charter actually functions as the project plan.

Now, if you have to do all this work in order to bid on a contract job in the first place, you might as well go with the comprehensive Project Charter approach, but otherwise we don't recommend this approach. (Although you must do what your organization requires of you, of course.) While each of these elements must eventually be prepared to make your project plan, you normally want to see if you can get approvals at each stage. Having to do it all before you find out that it's not what the customer wants means a lot of wasted work. And if someone needs a 50-page document before a project is approved, the incentive to do a project in the first place is lessened rather drastically.

Signed, Sealed, Delivered...It's Yours!

At each step in the project, you want to make sure that there is an understanding and a meeting of the minds before you move forward. Once there's an approved Project Charter and a SMART objective, the project is a reality. You've had your chance to provide influence and feedback on the project—and now, it's yours. This doesn't mean you'll never have to revisit any of this groundwork —major phases of a longer project often have to go through an Initiation stage and approvals for each of the phases—but it does signify that a major milestone is completed. You're ready to dig into the details.

Chapter 3:
Planning Your Project

PLANNING IS THE SECOND OF THE FIVE PROCESS GROUPS in project management. Because it involves the highest number of possibly unfamiliar skills, it takes up a large portion of this book—and of any other guide to project management. In this phase, you will encounter new tools and new ideas, all of which combine to put your project on the most solid footing possible.

The act of planning is often misunderstood. As a result, many who could get important benefits from planning fail to do so, either by not planning at all, or planning in too superficial a sense.

One common misunderstanding is that planning = scheduling. That is, a plan is simply a timeline of events. That is one part of a plan, but it's not all. We care about how long it will take, of course, but we also are interested in how much it will cost and what labor is required.

Another misunderstanding is that planning = certainty. That is, we start with an expectation that our plan describes what *will* happen on our project. While it's often desirable if our plan happens to play out exactly as scripted, in the real world of projects you often have such a degree of uncertainty that it's not a practical expectation.

Should you bother to plan if you don't have knowledge or control of many key project elements?

Absolutely. Planning is not about certainty, it's often about risk management. As our planning shows areas of risk, we can create responses and make contingency plans to help manage that risk. We can start our project with a reasonable appreciation of the likelihood of on-time, on-budget results. We can negotiate reasonable expectations.

Planning is about even more than that. You can plan for quality—how can we make sure the outcome is what we want and need? You can plan for communications—how do we keep people informed about progress? You can plan for change—how can we modify the project based on likely change requests?

Great skill in planning isn't the only talent of the perfect project manager, but it's an essential one. Let's look at this in more detail.

Why Plans May Be Useless—But Why Planning Is Essential

The military axiom, "No battle plan, no matter how well conceived, ever survives first contact with the enemy," has been variously attributed to Napoleon, von Moltke, von Clausewitz, and Murphy. Regardless, the saying strikes right to the heart of project planning.

However, the related quote, "Plans are useless, but planning is essential," comes from Dwight D. Eisenhower. Here's why this is true.

Plans are useless. First, the environment in which your project will take place is never completely knowable. There is inherent and unavoidable uncertainty in the business situation, resources, other demands and emergencies, and the attitude and focus of the people on whom you depend.

Second, the project itself carries inherent uncertainty. Does everyone really see the project in the same way? Do people seek the same outcomes? Will doing the project uncover problems unknowable in advance?

The upshot is that no matter how well or carefully you plan, you should never act on the assumption that you have thought of everything, and that nothing outside your carefully conceived universe will interfere.

What, then, is the value in planning?

Planning is essential. The most important value in planning is the work itself. By systematically thinking through and analyzing your project, you gain valuable knowledge and insight.

A proper attention to planning equips your mind with the tools to handle inevitable project problems. Even if a schedule slips, the plan informs you that the schedule has slipped, allows you to calculate the consequences, and gives you the opportunity to look down the path to see where other alterations might be possible, bringing you back on track.

Planning helps you learn the terrain. Stakeholder analysis tells you who the key players are and what their interests and likely actions will be with respect to the project. Risk planning lets you exercise likely what if scenarios, and provides you with a tool to manage the Godzilla Principle. Communications planning helps ensure that all those involved with a project are on the same page, and choose their actions with knowledge of their effect on the project. Quality planning tells you what customers value on your project, how to get there, and where the good enough point resides. Scope management planning helps you get agreement on what's in the project and what's not, and implements processes and systems to control scope creep throughout your project.

The project manager who plans has power. The project manager who does not plan is at the mercy of uncertain events.

The Devil Is in the Details

As important as a good Project Charter is to your project, it's only the beginning of what you need to manage your project in the most effective manner. By its nature, the Project Charter gathers and organizes high-level information about the project, and does not delve deeply into details. Unfortunately, the details *are* the project, and it's not infrequent that even with the best of intentions, important unknown details can drastically mutate or even destroy the project.

In areas like R&D, where outcomes are necessarily uncertain, the Project Charter is a license to get started, but no one should be surprised when you need to revisit the initial understanding based on the information you've gathered in the planning process.

At the first level of detail in the Planning phase of our project, we are trying to develop another document, this one known as the Scope Statement or Statement of Work. Whichever term you use (we'll use Scope Statement from now on), this is a more detailed description of the work and how it is to be completed. As in our discussion of the Project Charter, the format is less important than the substance.

Analyzing Project Scope

Getting something done may require a project, or it may require multiple projects, depending on its size and complexity. Sometimes, all the work necessary to accomplish the goal belongs to the project, but other times only part of the work is in the project; the rest is done by or supplied by someone else. The first part is the project scope, the second part is out of scope, even if it's very important. (You'll notice "in scope" and "out of scope" items in Figure 5, the Project Charter Template.)

Your operational responsibility is for the scope of the project, that is all of the products and services that are to be provided within the project. Others are responsible for out-of-scope activities. If they don't provide their work on a timely basis, it can have an impact on your ability to get your project done. If something crops up on the project that has not been anticipated, the question of whether it is in scope determines whether it's your problem or not.

The scope of the project includes a list of requirements that must be met, deliverables that must be completed, and responsibilities that are owned by the project.

If you don't define scope completely and in detail, you may find others attempting to shift their scope onto your project—one of the fundamental conditions leading to scope creep.

Assumptions and Constraints

Some aspects of project scope may not be known or understood at the beginning of the project. To help uncover hidden scope issues, develop a list of project assumptions and constraints.

Assumptions. In the absence of full knowledge or understanding of the project, it's common for project customers, sponsors, or stakeholders to make various assumptions. Typical assumptions might be that the technology exists to perform a certain action, or that the specialized resources you need will be available when you're ready, or that there is little or no risk in a particular activity.

One of the most powerful analytical things you can do is develop a list of the assumptions that people are making about the project. Unfortunately, some of the most problematic assumptions are formed and held on a subconscious level. The person making the assumption has made it on such a deep level that he or she is actually unaware that it is an assumption.

You can hold subconscious assumptions about the project as easily as anyone else, and it's very difficult to uncover one's own assumptions. Nevertheless, it's worth some self-examination to try and uncover them.

Assumptions come in three basic flavors: (1) assumptions that can be confirmed as true or false, (2) assumptions made for the sake of safety, and (3) assumptions that should be treated as risks.

Once you have a list of assumptions, inspect them. Confirm the ones you can. Not all assumptions, unfortunately, can be checked out in advance of doing the work. If whether the assumptions prove true or false will affect your project outcomes, they're risks. You'll address those alongside other risks later in the process.

If you find out some important assumptions are false, it's time to reopen dialogue with your stakeholders. If you have a long list of unverifiable assumptions, it's a good idea to let your project sponsor know that the project has a significant risk attached to it. Avoid surprising your management and customers whenever possible.

Some assumptions are made for safety reasons, and we treat them as true even if we're pretty sure they aren't. We wear our seat belts even though we're unlikely to be in an accident; we treat a gun as loaded even if it's probably not. As long as we're conscious that it's an assumption, that's fine.

Constraints. Your initial work has uncovered some of the constraints on your project, but further examination may find other obstacles. Not all constraints, as we've pointed out, are part of the Triple Constraint, but they can limit your options and sometimes mean that the project cannot be completed as initially intended.

Note that you can assume something is a constraint—not all assumptions are positive ones. You may believe that there is a big barrier to your success, but maybe it's just a question of perception.

Identifying Deliverables

People want you to do a project so you can satisfy a need or solve a problem. You want to give them a product or service that achieves the goal—but what exactly is that? The physical things or acts that you turn over to the customer are known as deliverables, because, well, you deliver them.

Each deliverable on a project will require the use of resources (e.g, staff time) and may involve the expenditure of money as well. As you can see, it's vital that you start your project with a comprehensive list of the deliverables. These in turn will be integrated into the plan, and you can verify that the work is done and the turnover is made for each deliverable in the process.

You'll see the deliverables list show up next in producing the Work Breakdown Structure (WBS).

Determining Project Requirements—Both Stated and Unstated

A popular definition of quality comes from the work of Philip Crosby who defined quality as "conformance to requirements." In other words, we first establish in detail what someone wants, and specify these items as a list of requirements. As we accomplish the deliverables, we ensure that each deliverable satisfies the requirements placed on it. If we've done that successfully, at the end of the project, quality should be a measurable fact.

From our list of deliverables and our understanding of the project, we must produce a set of requirements and make sure those requirements are agreed to by our customers, internal or external.

Requirements management is a life-of-the-project process, and it's one of the measurable, verifiable ways you can build quality into the project. People also play games with requirements; they can be a way to sneak scope creep into a project. You need to be concerned, therefore, not only with *what* the requirements of the project are, but also from *whom* the requested requirement comes. In the same way that you can be blindsided (either deliberately or inadvertently) by a deliverable you didn't know you had, you can also be blindsided by requirements that show themselves only after you've completed the work in question.

Discovering requirements. It's highly unusual on a project of even medium complexity for you to be presented with a perfect and complete requirements list at the beginning of your project. Many requirements are yet to be determined, and unfortunately some are assumed, and therefore not spelled out. Expect to do some digging to figure out your initial set of requirements, then circulate them around your stakeholders a couple of times to find out what you've missed. In the first round, you simply want input. Afterwards, you may want to inspect and weed out some requirements that may not belong.

Requirements can be located in many places: the Project Charter, the contract, applicable rules and regulations, systems engineering documentation, and more. Some requirements are interpolated; i.e., a requirement in one area may generate requirements in another.

Analyzing requirements. A requirement may be either functional (about how it works or what it does) or technical (an engineering description of a standard it must meet). Technical requirements should be rooted in functional ones—how does this technical requirement affect the customer?

Requirements need to be analyzed for assumptions and constraints, for technical issues and interpolated requirements, and for source and legitimacy.

Not everything labeled as a requirement is legitimately binding on you. If you don't check, you run a big risk by doing it (and finding out later you shouldn't have) or by not doing it (and finding out later that it was completely legitimate).

Requirements Allocation and Tracking. At the conclusion of this process, you want to have a detailed and written requirements list that has been approved by the key stakeholders for your project. This now becomes a measurable set of objectives for you and your team to meet.

Will requirements change? It's likely they will, and that becomes part of your change management system. Remember to ask for all changes in writing and always identify the consequences of making the change. If you've done this correctly, changes with big consequences for your project are easier to resist.

Why You Can Be Held Responsible for What They *Didn't* Tell You

By handling this process correctly, you want to put yourself in a position in which you are following an agreed-upon set of standards for your project that have objective measurements. If you achieve the standards, you have succeeded. If this process has not been performed well, then you may find yourself taken by surprise when you've done exactly what you think you're supposed to have done, and yet people are unhappy with the result. This usually means that there were some requirements or goals that you didn't know about.

Sometimes, that's your problem even if your customers or managers never told you about it. There are some objectives and requirements for which you are expected to have the judgment and knowledge to figure out on your own. In those cases, you are fully responsible whether you actually figured it out or not. To avoid this kind of problem, steep yourself in the context and circumstances of your project, and the organizational environment in which it takes place.

You can also see the consequences of failure at this stage. If you fail to properly identify assumptions and constraints, if you miss identifying some project deliverables, if you don't identify all the measurable requirements, you'll normally discover them late in your project, where the cost and time to get back on track may be prohibitive. Godzilla will have entered Tokyo!

The Work Breakdown Structure

A *scope statement* describes the project scope and deliverables. The next step in the planning process is to organize the project in terms of the work that must be performed to achieve the goal. This is called a Work Breakdown Structure, or WBS, and it's the first of the formal tools of project planning. Because the WBS is fundamental to all subsequent steps in the planning process, it's extremely important to do a good job.

The WBS can resemble either an organizational chart or an outline, and, as the name suggests, displays a breakdown of the project into its component activities, or tasks. If it's done correctly, all of the work necessary to accomplish the project is defined and shown. When all the WBS activities are completed, the project will be done.

The WBS will consist of a minimum of three levels; you may have more. The first level, which would be the CEO in a traditional org chart, represents the project itself. The second level represents the departments, phases, or—sometimes—subprojects in the project. You may arrange the work of your project in any organizational format that makes sense to you and meets your needs. The third level of the WBS consists of the actual work packages, known as activities. It is by doing these activities that the project gets accomplished.

What's challenging about the WBS is not so much the theory—it's pretty straightforward—but rather the importance of getting it right on the fine details. The work you did in developing the Project Charter and Scope Statement is all preparatory work for this stage.

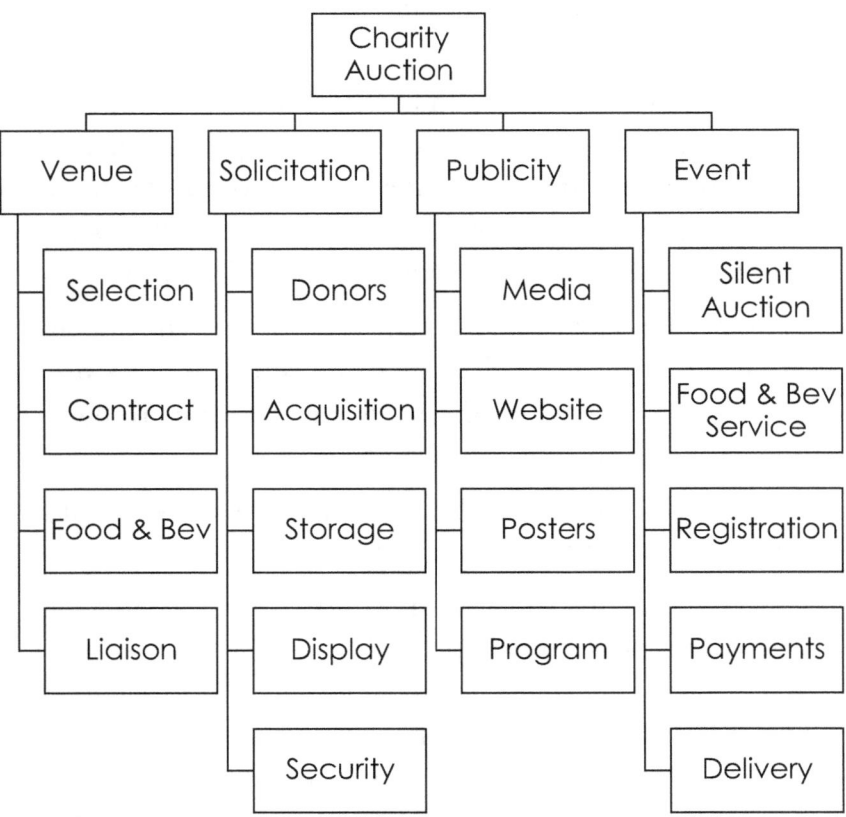

Fig 6. Work Breakdown Structure

Why the WBS Underlies All Steps in Planning

The WBS is used for project scheduling, estimating, risk management, change management, and communications with the customer and team member.

What do the project manager and the project team need to know in order to accomplish a project?

- A list of all the work packages and activities necessary to accomplish the project. What exactly must be done?

- A list of assigned responsibilities and accountabilities for each of the work packages and activities, grouped together for each organizational unit that will be working on the project. Who will do each job, and how will jobs be grouped together?

- A match of the project's requirements to the specific tasks and activities in which the requirements must be satisfied. How good does each task have to be to accomplish the overall project?

- A sequence in which the work is to be done. What comes first, and what comes next?

- What problems can we anticipate? Where will those problems occur in the project?

The WBS either accomplishes or serves as a foundation for accomplishing each of the objectives. It then serves as the technical or performance baseline for the project, allowing you to measure the amount of work accomplished.

A Task? Project? Program?

One thing you'll notice about a WBS is that some of the tasks can take a tremendous amount of effort, time, and money. If this task is assigned to a team, the team might well consider the assignment to be a project in its own right!

That's a perfectly legitimate way to look at the situation. The difference between a task, a project, and a program has some arbitrary elements to it, and you can use whichever term seems reasonable and appropriate to define *your* relationship to the work.

How Many Levels?

The WBS will have a minimum of three levels, but there isn't any official standard for how far down your WBS should be divided. There are a variety of different standards available—in one, tasks should be no more than 80 hours of effort; in another, tasks should represent from 0.5 to 2.5 percent of the total project. You have to do what makes sense for your own project. The WBS is a more flexible tool than some others in project management, because it must allow you to handle projects of any size and dimension.

The answer to whether you've broken your project down deeply enough has to do whether you and the team that has to do the work find that the job is *manageable*: that you can get your mind comfortably around it and that your team can get it done.

It doesn't matter if you see your work as a program and assign projects to subordinates, or if your boss sees your work as a task and your divisions as subtasks. If the choice of perspective helps you manage the work for which you are responsible, you've done the right thing.

The WBS and Cost Control. If you're going to go to the work and effort of maintaining a comprehensive single file of all tasks on a mammoth project, you need to have a benefit in mind that will repay the significant expense involved in building and maintaining it.

One of the values of a WBS is that it provides a method for cost accounting on a project. If you want to aggregate costs by cost centers, you can develop your WBS with that in mind. Each category in Level 2 can be a major cost account, so when you expend money, it will flow directly to the appropriate budget category, allowing detailed financial control of the project.

Developing a Work Breakdown Structure

There are two basic processes for building a WBS, known as the top down method and the bottom up method. The circumstances of your project will normally influence the choice you make; both are equally legitimate and effective.

Top Down Method. In the top down method of building a WBS, you normally start with the first two levels of your WBS already complete. Sometimes the initial project organizational structure is established by your company or by your customer; sometimes there's just one sensible way to set things up.

You start at the highest level and break down large pieces of the project into components. Different WBS categories may have different levels of breakdown: it doesn't have to be the same for each Level 2 category. One area may be broken down in very fine detail and another may consist of one or two large activities, and that's okay. As long as each area is something you and your team understand, you've done a fine job.

You won't necessarily have all the information to complete a top-to-bottom WBS for the project in a single meeting. Sometimes the executive summary level of the WBS gets done early by the senior team, and then the individual work groups go away to develop their detail lists. In a subsequent meeting, the details get combined back into a master project WBS.

Bottom up. On other projects, you don't start with a WBS Level 2 completed. A project may be so new that we don't have an organizational structure to handle it. You may want to consider a variety of approaches to the project.

Accordingly, in the bottom up technique, you and the team brainstorm as many different tasks as possible. Arguments and discussions are welcome, as this is a brainstorming event. Once you're satisfied that you have a comprehensive task list, then look for logical groupings, and build your WBS Level 2 backwards.

Don't forget anything...and don't put down what shouldn't be there. One important rule in constructing a WBS is that it is—by definition—the sum total of the project, i.e., if it's not in the WBS, it's not in the project!

Because all subsequent planning is based on the WBS, what if you've forgotten a task that is required? Unfortunately, the answer is that when you discover—too late—that the task is required, you've budgeted neither money, nor resources, nor time to get it done. This can be a project killer.

And because the WBS is a complete statement of project scope, if your WBS contains work you are not supposed to do, you're wasting money and time and may be treading on someone else's toes by doing it.

How can you be sure, then, that your WBS is complete and correct? Try these ideas:

Deliverables. Each deliverable for your project requires at least one task to get it done. (Some require more.) Take your list of deliverables and make sure the WBS contains all the work to get each deliverable completed.

Scope. Read the other project documents you've developed—Project Charter, Scope Statement, etc.— looking for indications that there is specific work required.

Reviews. Get others to review your WBS looking for what you may have missed. You can make it a game, offering a soda and candy bar to each person who catches you in a serious WBS omission.

Dual brainstorming teams. Divide your project team in two and have each one develop the project WBS separately. Compare the two for anything one team thought of that the other team missed.

Customer/sponsor approval. Have your WBS reviewed and approved by the customer and sponsor. They may not catch everything, but it's a little better for you if they missed it too.

When—and If—to Use Software

You can use your WBS in most popular project management software packages. You can enter the WBS and use it to organize activities in your final schedule. This can be useful on large projects (a hundred or more activities), but isn't hugely useful on small projects.

Project management software, however, is definitely not the tool of choice when it comes to constructing a WBS in the first place! You'll find that sticky notes and a whiteboard provide a much better method to assemble your original WBS as you brainstorm with your team. It's not unusual to rearrange the WBS a few times and that's the virtue of sticky notes. You and your team can brainstorm until you get it right.

When you finish your WBS, you, your team, and your stakeholders can visually appreciate what is involved in doing the project. There may be more work than you thought, or sometimes you find now that it's up where you can see it, it's not nearly so troublesome as you feared. Don't be in a hurry to lock down the WBS; make sure you've got it straight before you move on.

Building a Network Diagram

Our WBS gives us the tasks and a sense of who will do what, but we don't yet know the order in which the work will be done, or how long we should allow for each activity. That's why the next step in our process is to build a Network Diagram. You'll be glad you used sticky notes in building the WBS, because you can use them again to lay out your network. (Be sure to save your WBS in whatever form you choose, as you'll use it later.)

Create an Activity Table

Start by breaking down each WBS work package into the activities needed to accomplish it. For our charity auction WBS, let's start with the Venue category, with the Selection and Contract elements. Figure 7 lists the necessary activities to accomplish the work.

Write each activity on a separate sticky note.

Arrange Activities in a Flow Chart

A network diagram is essentially a flowchart of the work of the project, and uses many familiar elements. Create a sticky note labeled "Start," then lay out the activities in a logical order. Finish with a sticky note labeled "Finish," and connect the notes with arrows. Eventually you'll need to estimate how long each will take and how much it will cost, but for now the sequence is enough. Figure 8 shows an example.

WBS Element	Activity
Selection	Establish criteria
	Identify potential venues
	Inspect properties
	Review responses
	Select venue
Contract	Prepare and send RFP
	Negotiate contract
	Sign contract

Fig 7. Activity List

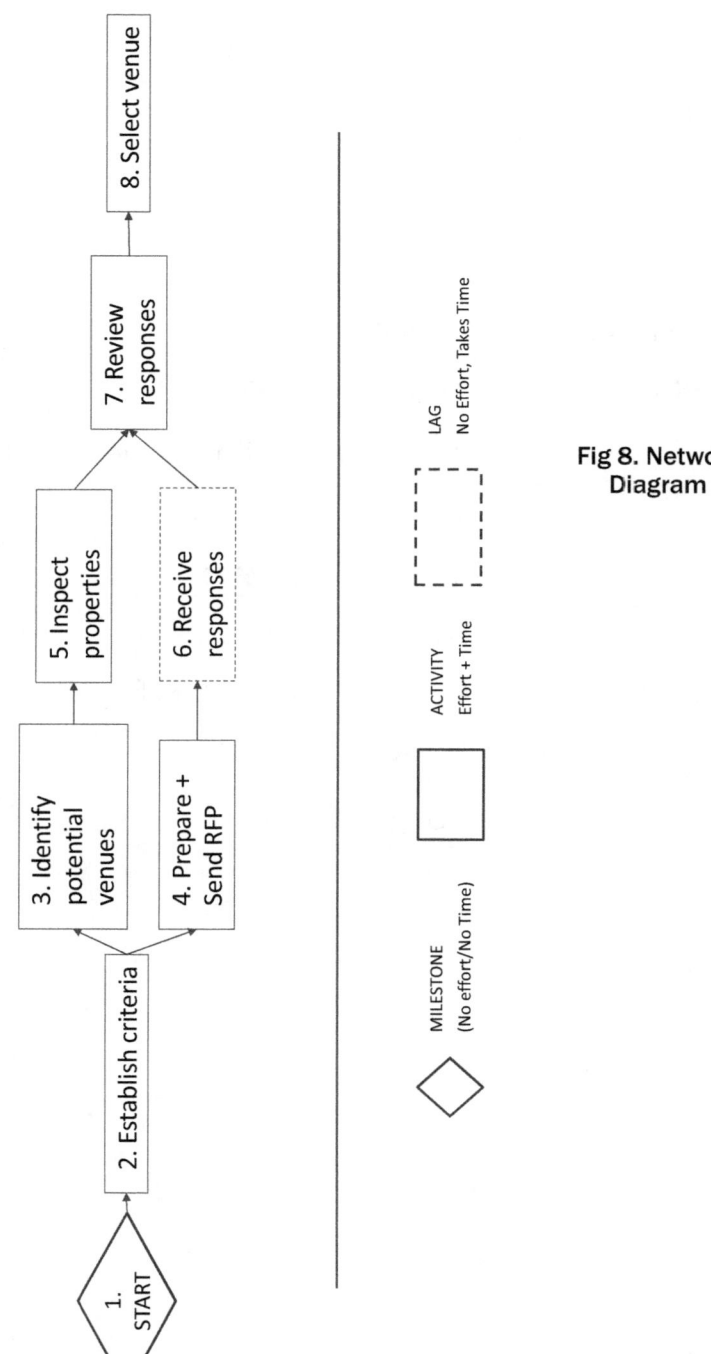

Fig 8. Network
Diagram

Understanding Dependencies

The way to read Figure 8 is that each activity *depends* on its predecessor(s). The activity "Establish criteria" must *finish* before either "Identify potential venues" or "Prepare and send RFP" can *start*. That's called a "finish-to-start" relationship. It's by far the most common, but it's not the only type of *dependency relationship*. You should know about three types of dependencies.

Finish-to-Start (FS) dependency. You need to *finish* Task 1 before you can *start* Task 2. This is the most common type of dependency, and it's normally assumed as the default dependency, especially in project management software.

Start-to-Start (SS) dependency. Imagine that you plan to manufacture 1,000 widgets and then put them in boxes. Do you have to wait until all 1,000 widgets are done to put the first in a box? No, not at all. There's probably some minimum number of widgets that need to be completed before it makes sense to start the boxing process, and the final widget can't be put into a box until it has been manufactured. But you can drastically shorten the calendar time if you use a Start-to-Start (SS) dependency: the *start* of Task 2 depends on the *start* of Task 1, with a slight lag to allow the first (say) 100 widgets to be completed before boxing starts.

Finish-to-Finish (FF) dependency. In cooking Thanksgiving dinner, you normally work backwards from the scheduled mealtime, and figure out when to start each dish so that they will all finish at the same time, and be hot when brought to the table. That's an example of a

Finish-to-Finish dependency, in which the *finish* of Task 2 is dependent on the *finish* of Task 1, with or without lag or lead times.

While you'll use FS dependencies the vast majority of the time, it can be very helpful to know about this when you're trying to make your schedule efficient.

Strategic Choices in Task Relationships

You don't always have a choice about the order in which the tasks of your project must be done. In the sequence Dig Hole →Pour Concrete, there's only one feasible way to do it.

Other times, there are a lot of possible choices. When that's the case, explore them all. Each will affect your project in different ways, and you can choose the answer the suits your needs best. Figure 9 shows your options:

Putting the Diagram Together

Start by making a new sticky note and labeling it "Start." Put it up on your whiteboard or flip chart. Make a second new sticky note, label it "Finish" and put it at the very end of the board. Now, ask yourself (and your team if you're doing this together) what activities can be started at the beginning of your project. Take those sticky notes from your WBS and put them to the right of the "Start" node. Draw arrows from the "Start" node to the sticky notes you've placed.

FS Dependency (B is dependent on A)

Activities B and C are dependent on Activity A; activities B and C are parallel to each other.

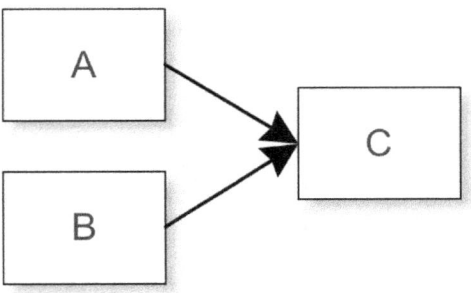

Activities A and B are parallel to each other; Activity C is dependent on the finish of both A and B.

Fig 9. Dependency Relationships

Now, for each sticky note that follows "Start," ask yourself (and your team), "What activities can start once this task is complete?" Put those sticky notes after the activity you've chosen, and draw arrows from that task to the new tasks. Work left to right until all the tasks from your WBS have been placed into a network. Draw arrows from the last tasks to the "Finish" node.

You've now created a Network Diagram for the project. Let's review the rules and guidelines.

Rules for Network Diagramming

1. We began by creating a sticky note with "Start" written on it. That's necessary when more than one

task can begin at the kickoff of the project. It's optional

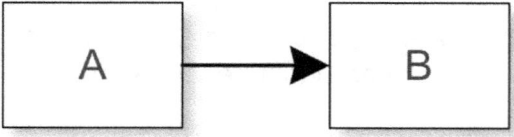

(though still a good practice) when only one task starts

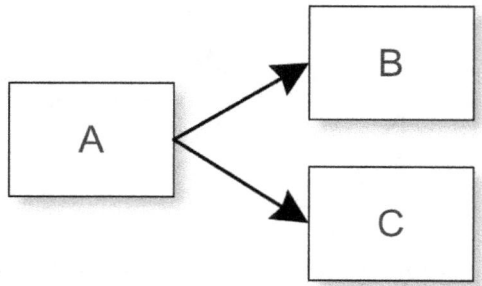

a project.

2.   That's the sticky note marked "Finish." That's necessary when more than one task live at the end of the project, optional (but good practice) if not.

3.   For every activity (except "Start," of course), there must be at least one line coming into it from a previous task. The predecessor/dependency relationship may be any of the types we've discussed (FS, SS, FF).

4.   For every activity (except "Finish," of course), there must be at least one line coming out of it and going to a subsequent task. This successor/dependency relationship may be any of the types we've discussed.

5.   In regular flowcharting, loops are extremely common. You might find them useful in this kind of charting because some project tasks may have to be done

multiple times. The reason you cannot is that these relationship also signal forward movement in time—in the absence of a time machine, loops can't exist in project plans.

Finding the Critical Path

The **critical path** is the longest path through a schedule network; a sequence of activities from the project start to finish, all of which have slack or float less than or equal to zero.

Total Slack/Float. The extra time available to finish a task before it results in a delay to the project.

Free Slack/Float. The extra time available to finish a task before it delays its successor task, whether or not the project is delayed as a result.

Duration. The number of work days (or other periods) necessary to complete a task or project. Does not count nonworking days, such as weekends or holidays.

Calendar time. The number of calendar days (or other periods) necessary to complete a task or project. Includes weekends, holidays, or other non-working days.

Effort. The number of work hours necessary to complete a task or project. If someone is not working full time on a task or project, the level of effort will be less than the duration. If someone is working full-time or overtime, or if more than one person is working full-time on the task or project, the level of effort can be greater than the duration.

In Figure 12, we return to our charity auction, adding durations to each activity. How long will it take to get the project done?

Note there are two different paths through this project. One is 1-2-3-5-7-8, and the other is 1-2-4-6-7-8. Add up the durations for each. For 1-2-3-5-7-8, we get 29 days; for 1-2-4-6-7-8 it's 26. Because all the work has to be completed, the longest path (the critical path) of 29 days is the planned duration of the project.

While any slippage in a critical path activity automatically means the project will be late; activities with slack or float have some extra time. Compare the path segment 3-5 (20 days) with segment 4-6 (17 days). If activities 4 and 6 take up to three days (combined) more than scheduled, your deadline is unchanged. The slack in activity 4 is not free, because if 4 goes late, 6 ends up with less slack. The slack in 6 is free, because it doesn't delay any other task.

Using Project Slack as a Resource

Slack is your friend, if you know how to treat it right.

There's one automatic and obvious advantage to having slack; it lowers the consequence to the project if that task should slip over schedule. You don't have a deadline problem unless the slippage becomes greater than the amount of slack available. (Of course, it's possible for you to have a budget problem—slack helps the time constraint but does nothing for the cost constraint.

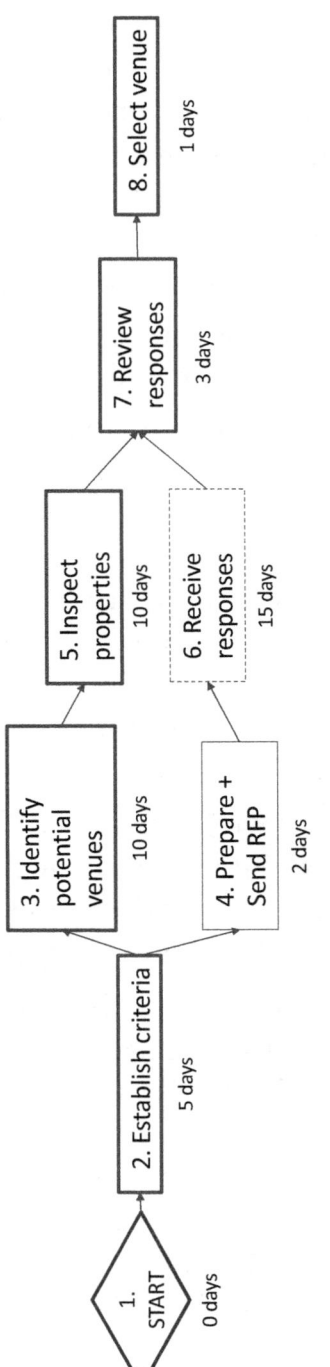

Fig 10. Network Diagram With Durations

As a project manager during project execution, you may be able to afford to pay less attention to activities with plenty of slack. If some of the members of your team are faster (or slower) than others, you might consider putting the faster ones on critical path activities and the slower ones on tasks with slack.

Slack as a project resource. But most importantly, slack can in some circumstances turn into an extra project resource. Let's go back to our system installation project.

We know there are two days of slack available in Task 3 "Select Hardware." But if you've assigned a full-time project team member to that job, you have two extra days to play with. You can do a variety of things. You can assign the person to another project for those two days. You can increase the performance standard for the task. You can keep the two days in reserve in case of emergencies. Notice you can only do *one* of these things— once the two days are spent, they're gone.

Imagine that something goes wrong in Task 2 "Select Software." That's on the critical path, and so if it goes late, the bumper car effect is going to push out the deadline. Where can you get help? Slack to the rescue!

There are three possibilities (assuming that the Task 3 resource has the technical skills to be of use on Task 2 and that Task 2 is the kind of job where extra hands can speed it up—neither are always the case): 1) You can wait until Task 3 is done, and shift the resource into Task 2 for the remaining two days. 2) You can delay the start of Task 3 (move it from its ES to its LS date) and invest the two days in Task 2 up front. (While this might increase risk in Task 3, it could be worth it.) 3) You can interrupt Task 3 in the middle, and shift the person up to Task 2.

While in some circumstances you can compress your project so there is no slack left, you may not want to do that, especially if there is a significant degree of risk or uncertainty about the project. Keep a little something up your sleeve in case of emergencies.

Developing a Gantt Chart

For the majority of small to medium-size projects, the Gantt Chart is the most frequently used planning tool. Although it has some limitations, it's still a very practical tool, useful in scheduling, resource management, milestone planning, and tracking. In its various special forms it can serve as an aid to delegation, a briefing and summarizing chart for senior management and customers who don't necessarily have an understanding of project management mechanics, and much more.

From Network Diagram to Gantt Chart

To build a Gantt chart either manually or by computer, you need the following information:

- A list of all the activities in your project
- The duration of each activity
- Dependency relationships of each activity

You develop the list of tasks in building your WBS, then you develop dependency relationships in constructing your network diagram. After you estimate duration of each task, you enter that information into your network diagram. As a result, you should be able to organize all the Gantt chart information by referring to your Network Diagram. Figure 13 turns the network diagram in Figure 12 into an activity table. Notice there is no new information here; it's just putting the data in a new format.

By the way, if you are using project management software, all you will have to do is type this information directly into the appropriate fields of the program.

Task Number	Task Name	Duration	Predecessors
1	Start	0 days	None
2	Establish criteria	5 days	1
3	Identify potential venues	10 days	2
4	Prepare and send RFP	2 days	2
5	Inspect properties	10 days	3
6	Receive responses	15 days	4
7	Review responses	3 days	5,6
8	Select venue	1 day	7

Fig 11. Activity Table

How to Draw a Gantt Chart

One of the functions of project management software programs is the creation of Gantt charts. A Gantt chart is basically a bar graph drawn over a calendar grid, and is a common and very effective way to display and manage a schedule.

While you can use project management software to do this, you don't have to. If the project is small, or you don't have access to project management software, a sheet of graph paper and a straightedge will do the trick. Many drawing programs have Gantt chart templates, and you can even create one with a spreadsheet program — which is what we've done in Figure 12.

All the information you need to create a Gantt chart comes from your activity table.

Start the Gantt Chart by listing the tasks in order down the left side. Put a time scale across the top, because a Gantt Chart displays work over time. Because we're only considering duration (work days), not calendar time (including weekends and holidays), and because it's a small project, we're using a scale of one block equals two days. For a longer, more complex project, each block can represent a longer duration (e.g., 1 week).

The first task is "Start," and as you remember, that's a milestone because it has zero duration. Now, it's tough to draw a line of zero width and have it easily seen. So, the Gantt Chart convention is to represent a milestone with a diamond (♦). This particular milestone starts the project, so it goes in the very first block at the left edge.

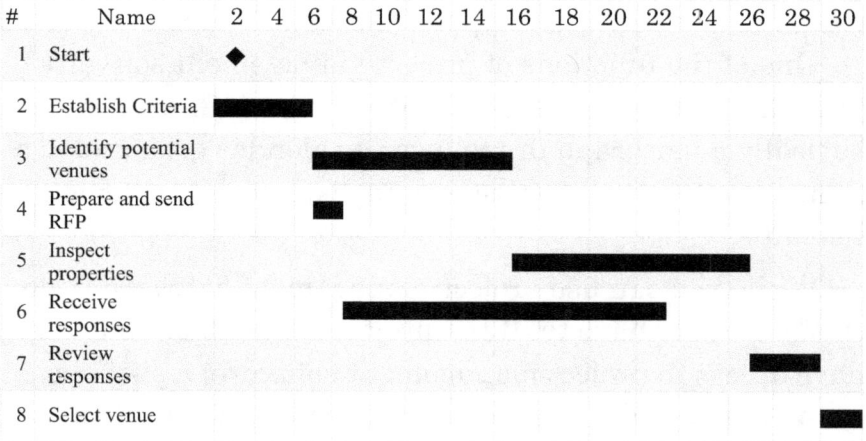

Fig 12. Gantt Chart

The second task is "Establish criteria." It's dependent on "Start," which means that its bar starts exactly where "Start" ends. In this case, since "Start" is a milestone, "Select Software" also starts at the beginning of the project. It has a duration of 5 days, so draw a line from the left edge of the first block to the middle of the 6 block. Voila! You've now shown graphically the task's duration and start and finish times.

Task 3 is "Identify potential venues." It has a duration of 10 days and is dependent on activity 2, "Establish criteria." So, draw a line from the center of block 6 (directly beneath the end of the "Establish criteria" bar) all the way to the middle of block 16. Figure 14 shows the completed Gantt chart.

Do remember that if an activity has more than one predecessor (like activity 7), it begins after the end of whichever predecessor ends latest. If you're using dependencies other than FS, use logic to draw the associated lines. If you're using software, it'll do that automatically as long as you mark the dependency appropriately. (If activity 4 has "3FF" in the Predecessor field, the bar begins where activity 3 ends, but goes backward. If it's "3SS+2d," the activity 4 bar begins two days after its predecessor starts.

Compressing the Schedule

In your first draft of a Gantt chart, don't worry about the deadline. Your first goal is to figure out what kind of shape you're in. Maybe you don't have a scheduling problem at all. If you do, a Gantt chart is a good way to see how to fix it.

There are numerous ways to shorten a project schedule. While not every technique works in every situation, it's worth considering all your options.

By the way, if the project has an unbreakable deadline, I plan my schedule to finish early, so there's some safety margin in case things slip.

Here are some tips to compress your project schedule.

Shorten individual critical path task times

The most obvious way to compress your schedule is to alter the estimates for individual tasks. It's only helpful to do this on the critical path, because if you shorten a non-critical task, all you get is more slack/float. Of course, you can't change an estimate unless you have a legitimate reason to justify it. Consider these possibilities:

1. If you add resources (people, equipment, money) to a task, it can sometimes shorten the expected duration. First, make sure you have the resources available when you need them. Second, you usually need a plan for how you will use the extra resources. Extra resources don't always speed things up. While two bricklayers may get the wall built in half the time, two pilots won't get the plane to its destination any faster (though arguably safer) and two systems designers may actually take longer to do the job than one!

2. Another way to make a task take less time is to do less work. Are there luxuries or nonessentials that can be cut or scaled back if time is tight? Are there elements that can be added to the final product at a later stage, when more resources and time may be available?

3. Time is not always the Driver of your project. Resources and performance may be more important. If that's the case, perhaps you can simply plan on a later finish.

Alter dependency relationships to make more activities parallel

When dependency relationships change, always check to see if the critical path has changed. If we make the change, will we simply make a new critical path? If so, we may not necessarily end up any better off than before.

Realize that changing dependency relationships may alter the way tasks are done, forcing you to alter your estimates. Again, until we do the arithmetic, we can't be sure if that cancels out the advantages.

Realize that not all dependency relationships can be changed. We know we can't pour the concrete for our swimming pool until the hole has been dug, no matter how convenient that might be. Make sure you can develop a strategy for getting the work done within the proposed change.

Use dependency types other than Finish-to-Start (FS)

So far, we've used FS dependencies throughout the project, but that's not necessarily the best way to go But perhaps not *all* of one task must be completed for a dependent task to begin. Maybe a Start-to-Start (SS) dependency with a lag of, say, 50 percent would work.

Assigning Resources to Tasks

All activities except for lag activities (like "Receive responses") require resources: people, money, tools, equipment, supplies, information, etc. You must assign the necessary resources to each activity, making sure that you not only have enough resources, but you have them *when* you need them. Because some activities happen in parallel, it's all too easy to find you've accidentally assigned the same person to overlapping activities.

The process of assigning resources to activities is known as *resource loading*. The process of identifying and resolving any resource conflicts is known as *resource leveling*.

Resource Availability

The first step is to see what you have available and match it to the work that needs to be done. If you don't have all the resources you need, you'll have to figure out how to get them or how to make do.

In this section, we'll focus on people. Allocating your budget to work packages and activities will be covered later.

Person	Role	Skills	Availability
Moe	Project Manager	Contracting, finance	25% (10 hours/week); full time last 5 days
Larry	Team Member	Event management	25% (10 hours/week); full time last 5 days
Curly	Team Member	Auctioneer, logistics	25% (10 hours/week); full time last 5 days
Shemp	Team Member	Marketing, event managemen	25% (10 hours/week); full time last 5 days

Fig 13. Resource Availability Table

Figure 13 organizes the necessary information into a table: the person, that person's project role, relevant skills, and availability.

Because this project is an additional duty, and all team member have regular jobs, they are not supposed to spend more than 25% of their time on this project, but they can work full time on the five days prior to the event. (Note, however, that they can spend 10 hours/week of their official 40 hours on the project, but no one says they can't work some voluntary overtime if they choose to,)

While many project management books suggest the project manager is a full time role, in practice (and especially on smaller projects) you're more likely to be a "working" project manager, meaning that you perform specific activities as well as provide overall management. If that's your situation, don't schedule yourself for the most difficult activities on the critical path. You need to be available where you're needed, so keep some flexibility to allow you to do the project management role.

While you may have some flexibility in choosing team members, it's limited. Your team is who you get, whether they're who you would have chosen or not. Even if you know your team members, interview them in terms of the project needs, especially if the project is outside the normal work of your department — like a charity auction. You may find some surprises. Who knew that Curly used to be an auctioneer?

Also check about other commitments. You're supposed to have ten hours per week from each team member, but they may have other commitments. Poor Shemp has been assigned to work 10 hours a week on six different projects. Unfortunately, two of them have impending deadlines during your project period, meaning it's very likely Shemp won't be nearly as available as planned.

Skill Availability

According to Figure 13, you've got the following skills available: contracting, finance, event management, auctioneering, and marketing. How do those skills match up with your project needs? Figure 14 lists skill requirements by activity.

No.	Name	Skills Needed	Options
1	Start	Milestone	N/A
2	Establish criteria	Event management, logistics. finance	Full team
3	Identify potential venues	Event management	Larry, Shemp
4	Prepare and send RFP	Event management, contracting	Moe, Larry or Shemp
5	Inspect properties	Event management, logistics	Larry or Shemp,Curly
6	Receive responses	Lag activity	N/A
7	Review responses	Event management, logistics. finance	Full team
8	Select venue	Contracting	Full team, Moe

Fig 14. Skill Needs and Availability

Loading and Leveling the Gantt Chart

We're fortunate that Larry has event management skills, because we have reason to worry about Shemp's availability. Later in the project, as we start promoting the event, Shemp's marketing skills will become increasingly important, meaning we have to keep an eye on his availability. Perhaps we can bargain with other project managers to use less of Shemp's time in the early stages of the project to gain more availability later.

Moe, the project manager, has only two activities where his contracting skills are required: preparation of the RFP and the contracting process once the venue is chosen. That gives him flexibility in dealing with any issues.

In some projects, especially ones with multiple parallel activities, you may find that you have to shift activities in order to have resources available to get them done. Sometimes you'll then discover that shifting the activity just moves the problem elsewhere in your project, so always work from left to right, resolving each conflict as it occurs and adjusting the schedule if necessary before moving to the next conflict.

When you've got a resource conflict that needs to be leveled, here are some options:

- Move one of the conflicting activities to the right until there's a resource available to do the work. Notice that this could extend the finish date.

- If it's possible to move a conflicting activity into a part of your project with slack/float or a lag activity, you may be able to shift the schedule without pushing out the finish date.

- Reassign one of the conflicting activities to a different resource (possibly getting someone from outside the core project team).

- Depending on the level of difficulty, assign the activity to someone of lesser skill and provide coaching or other support.

- Use overtime.

Managing Excess Resources

Sometimes you'll find that there are parts of your project in which some of your team members have nothing to do. If the gap is small, that's okay. When things go wrong, you have some unallocated resources handy.

If the gap is large (weeks or months), you'll have to find something else for that person to do. If they have a regular job, they can go back to it. You may be able to barter availability with other project managers, and maybe get access to needed resources later on.

In a multiple project environment, technical specialists often do the same work for first one project, then the next. Sometimes, it may appear as if you have excess resources in your schedule, but if that excess resource time is already scheduled on another project, it's already gone. You can't spend it twice.

Old School Project Management

The Gantt chart, invented around 1910 by early management consultant Henry Gantt, is one of the oldest project management tools and is still one of the most widely used techniques. It's worth the effort to get comfortable and familiar with the tool. Whether you do a chart by hand for a small project or push the limits of your project management software, you'll find that for understanding the timeline and for the nuts-and-bolts of resource planning and resource management, it's enormously helpful.

Even if you plan to do your charting mostly on a computer, it's a good idea to practice doing a few by hand. The more you understand how the chart works, the better you'll understand what the computer is doing and how you can use it.

Planning for Project Risks

Because not everything is ever under your complete control, risk is an unavoidable aspect of project management. The discipline of risk management doesn't pretend that it can provide you with an absolute security blanket. Uncertainty and probability can be tamed to some extent, but completely caged, almost never. Still, with our project manager's motto of "Better is better," even a partial solution to the dilemma of risk is better than none.

Categories of Risk

A risk is not a problem. This distinction is at the heart of the Godzilla Principle. "Risk" is future tense; "problem" present. If you have developed a list of potential risk events for your project, some may occur, others not. And a few items not on your risk list may show up like an unexpected dinner guest!

The basic methodology for risk management is advance preparation. Some potential solutions are possible only if thought of well in advance. You might think of them when the risk turns into a problem, but it's too late. You're OBE, "Overtaken by Events." In addition, surprise disasters tend to create stress, if not downright panic, and for most of us, panic doesn't increase our intelligence or judgment.

The Triple Constraints and Risk Management

A risk is not merely an uncertain event. It has a specific type of impact on your project: it impacts the Triple Constraints. The three kinds of risks are those that (1) threaten to delay your project (Time risk), (2) threaten to increase your use of money and other resources (Cost risk), or (3) threaten to degrade the quality or functionality of the deliverables (Performance risk). (It can, of course, hit more than one of the three simultaneously.) If the risk you're considering won't do any of those things, it's not a risk—it's merely an event.

The potential seriousness of a risk, then, is influenced based on which Triple Constraint(s) it affects. If a risk threatens your Driver, it's far more serious than if the risk threatens your Weak Constraint. So, the Triple Constraints suggest a risk response strategy: exploit the Weak Constraint. If Cost is the Weak Constraint, your first thought for many risks should be, "Can spending money fix this?" If it's Time, "Can letting the project finish slip fix this?" And if it's Performance, "What can I drop or modify to fix this?"

Business risk vs. Insurance risk

Another way to divide risks is between business risks and insurance (or pure) risks. A business risk has the opportunity for gain as well as for loss. A stock market investment is an example of business risk. You might think of risks as generally something to avoid, but business risks are sometimes actively chosen for their upside potential.

An insurance, or pure, risk is one that only has the opportunity for loss. If you're running a construction project, there's the chance that a worker will be injured, or that a wall will collapse. Because the outcome is only negative, you want to avoid the risk if feasible. One obvious strategy for managing an insurance risk is to buy insurance. You'll need to distinguish between these two types of risk in developing your strategy.

Good luck vs. Bad luck

Risk management includes maximizing positive outcomes as well as minimizing negative ones. If you're managing a project that has business risk, you know there are opportunities for gain and for loss. If you can minimize either the chance of loss or the amount of loss, that's good for the project. Similarly, it's worth thinking how you could maximize the chance for gain or the amount of gain.

While insurance risk is always negative, there also exists the possibility of good luck and positive opportunity on your project. We frequently don't take the time to walk through our project plan and ask ourselves, "Could we get some good luck on this task, and if so, how?" You might be surprised.

Murphy's Law notwithstanding, we would expect random events to distribute themselves more or less evenly between good luck and bad luck, but that's not our operational experience. We seem to experience negative random events on projects much more commonly than positive ones. What's the reason?

One reason is that there is a structural difference in the way the two types of luck operate.

Bad luck is automatic. If you lose, say, $100, it requires no additional effort on your part to suffer the consequences. Good luck, on the other hand, often requires a deliberate effort on your part to gain its value. If there's $100 laying on the street, you might not notice it's there. If you do notice, you're under no actual obligation to pick it up. You might be suspicious that it's a trick of some sort. It might be raining. You might be in a hurry. And if you do pick up the $100, you're under no obligation to spend it wisely. You only get the benefit of the $100 as a result of deliberate, conscious action.

That has implications for project management, as well. Ignoring the opportunities good luck may provide is wasteful. When analyzing risks, take a little time to consider the upside, too.

Managing Risk Tolerance

Imagine that you're offered a stock market investment. Invest $5,000, and within six months, you will either receive $50,000 (70 percent chance) or lose the $5,000 (30 percent chance). Interested? Assuming the facts check out (and we'll assume they do for the purpose of this example), it looks like a pretty good deal.

The *expected monetary value* (EMV) of this transaction balances the upside and downside risks. It's based on the fundamental formula of risk: the value of a risk is the likelihood it will occur (probability) times its impact if it does occur (R=PxI).

$$R = P \times I$$

The value of a risk is the probability times the impact.

Fig 15. Fundamental Formula of Risk

We have two possibilities: gain or loss, so we need to do a PxI calculation for each side and add the numbers together. (Note that the chance of either winning or losing is 70%+30%, or 100%. The sum of the probabilities of all potential outcomes is, by necessity, always 100%.) Here is the EMV calculation.

$$EMV = (.7 \times \$50,000) + (.3 \times -\$5,000) =$$
$$EMV = \$35,000 + (-\$1,500) =$$
$$EMV = \$33,500$$

Fig 16. Expected Monetary Value (EMV)

In other words, if you made this investment over and over again, winning and losing according to the percentages, you would earn an average of $33,500 per transaction.

If you're an experienced investor and you've got $5,000 in your portfolio looking for a higher-risk/higher-gain investment, then you'd probably jump at this offer (after, of course, due diligence to make sure it is what it's represented to be).

In surveys, however, most people will turn this offer down. This isn't necessarily irrational. Imagine that the $5,000 you'd have to put up is the mortgage and family food budget for next month. Even though that $50,000 looks very attractive, you can't take the risk.

Tolerance for risk is a complicated issue. Personal tolerance for risk is partly a matter of style and emotional preference and partly determined by your circumstances and the effect of gains and losses. While there's nothing inappropriate about emotions, personal circumstances, and style preference playing a role, examine your own biases and tendencies to ensure that your final risk decisions really are those that are best for you.

In your role as project manager, you'll also have to take into account your organization's tolerance for risk, which may be greater or less than your own, or vary by category.

Discovering organizational tolerance for risk isn't always easy. Some managers talk a good game of taking risks and seizing opportunities. Unfortunately, when failure happens as a result of risk-taking, they look for the easiest victim to shoot for it. Other managers urge more caution, but are actually willing to accept intelligent risk-taking in a more positive spirit. Ask about risk tolerance, but also observe actual response to risk events and consequences.

In general, your job is to conform to the risk tolerance of your organization. There are, however, circumstances in which following normal procedure will lead to bad results, so you may need to push back in some instances.

How to Determine Your Project Risks

Figure 17 (next page) shows the steps in a formal risk management process.

Risk Management Planning. Overall policy and approach as it applies to your project.

Risk Identification. This is the process of identifying potential risks on the project.

Risk Analysis. For the identified risks, assess the probability and the impact to determine which risks are worth action.

Risk Response Planning. For the risks you decide are worth action, develop potential responses, either with preventive or corrective actions or contingency plans.

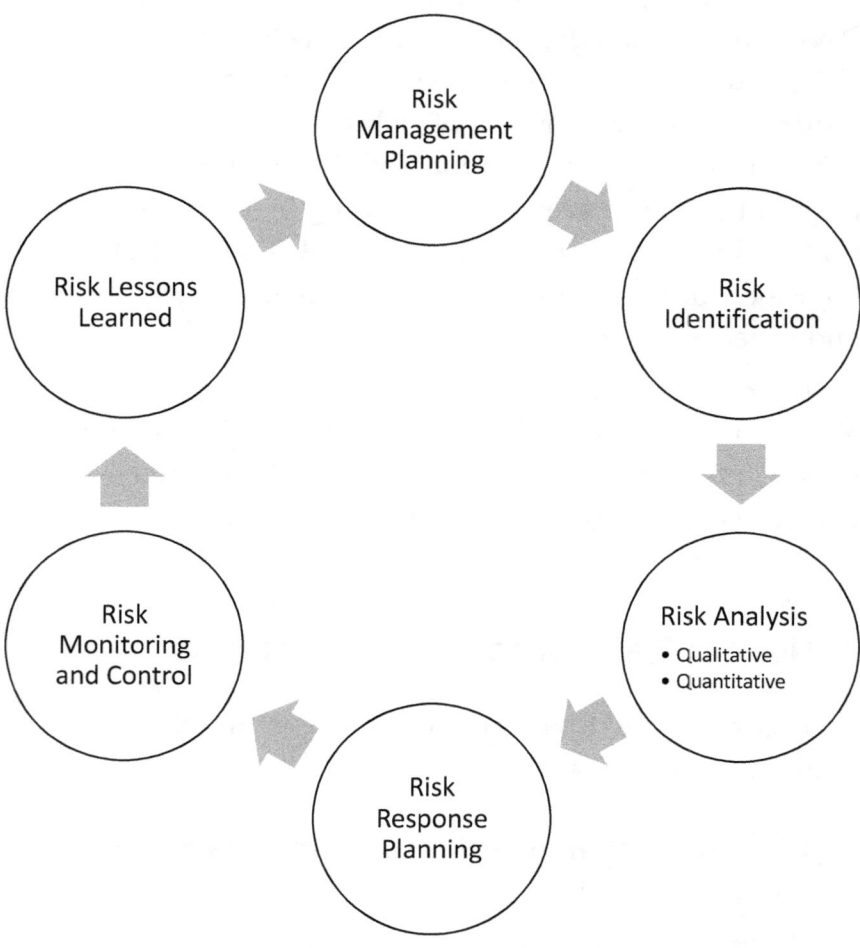

Fig 17. Risk Management Process

Risk Monitoring and Control. In the execution phase of your project, implement the plans that you have developed.

Risk Lessons Learned. Gather information and tools that can benefit future projects.

All these steps must be performed throughout the project life cycle, because some risks drop in significance and others rear their ugly heads for the first time within the project. As this section is all about risk management planning, we'll begin with risk identification.

Risk Identification

Not all the risks—even the really big risks—are necessarily obvious from a first glance at the project. It's good practice to make the process of risk identification methodical. Follow the processes described below to help identify risks. It's important to remember that each of these methods has biases and limitations. The more different techniques you use, the better the result will be.

Document analysis. Even in fairly early stages of the planning work, you are already amassing a number of documents that will facilitate your risk planning. These include any contractual documents, the Project Charter, Scope Statement/Statement of Work, and any correspondence with the customer.

Depending on the technical area of your project, you might also have systems engineering documentation, life-cycle cost analysis, and industry-specific risk management information from which to draw. It's worth it to do a little digging to discover these resources.

Interviews. Interview your stakeholders on risk issues. Customers, project sponsors, team members, and other affected parties can address the risk identification process from their own points of view. While all risks affect the underlying project, different stakeholders may be more or less affected by the same risk, and as a result can focus on the ones most important to them.

In addition, interview project managers who have done similar projects, technical experts on the disciplines that are part of your project (especially those that may be outside your own areas of expertise). Also interview sponsors and other senior managers in your own organization to determine issues of risk tolerance and policy implications.

Assumptions analysis and brainstorming. In the preparation of your Project Charter, you identified a list of constraints and assumptions. The assumptions—those that you weren't able to resolve into facts—also become risks for your consideration.

Part of your risk meeting work should be brainstorming about possible risks. This is a good way to identify global project risks. Like with all brainstorming, accept all suggestions uncritically and analyze them only after the brainstorming period has passed.

Plan analysis. The stages of your planning process also have risk implications. Some risks are global—they affect the entire project, or can happen at any time. Others are specific—they appear within a specific task or activity. As a result, analyze your WBS for risk. In each task, what could go wrong? How would it affect the project?

Network diagramming and the scheduling process have risk implications as well. When you make strategic choices about how to set up your network diagram, you will find that the different options have different consequences.

Risks involving tasks along the Critical Path are made more serious because any delay in one of those tasks immediately delays your project completion. Risks on tasks involving slack may be at least partially mitigated because a certain amount of delay has no project deadline consequences.

Write each risk on a *risk register* (figure 18). You'll fill in additional information as you get it. Note that risks should be written in an "if...then" format. If [condition] occurs, then [consequences]." You need both pieces of information if you're going to make informed risk decisions on your project.

ID	Risk Statement	Category	P	I	Rank	Action	Status
1	If Shemp's other projects take too long, he will not be available for our project as needed	Personnel	H	L	Yellow	Negotiate with other project mgrs	

Fig 18. Risk Register

Risk Analysis

Before you act on risks, you need to understand them. In classical (non-project) risk, the tools of *quantitative risk analysis* (statistics) are most commonly used. In project management, however, when we usually don't have the Law of Large Numbers on our side, the opportunity to use statistical or financial analysis tools are limited. Instead, we use *qualitative risk analysis*, a less formal (and less precise) method of assessing risk.

Quantitative Risk Analysis

One goal of risk analysis is concerned with measuring the seriousness of the risks you have identified. Not all risks rise to the threshold where a response is necessary. It's just not realistic to mitigate every conceivable risk on a project.

Here's where R=PxI comes into play. If there's a machining error of greater than 1/1000" in our manufacturing process, the final product will fail its quality control test. If there's a 10 percent chance (based on our history machining that kind of part) of this occurring, and the cost of a product failure is $15,000, then the risk score is 10% x $15,000, or $1,500. If buying a new lathe that has better reliability costs $5,000, and we don't need it for other work, then it's probably better to accept the risk of product failure.

Of course, that's not an absolute. There could be other consequences of product failure that we can't easily quantify, and if so, we might choose to make the investment in a new lathe anyway. For example, we might feel that our reputation for no-fail quality is important enough to justify the extra expense.

Qualitative Risk Analysis

In qualitative risk analysis, we sort the risks from the risk register based on their probability, impact, and route them for further action. Figure 19 shows the process in flowchart form; Figure 20 gives you action options.

Fig 19. Qualitative Risk Management Flowchart

For any given risk, there are really only three choices: accept the risk, transfer it to someone else, or do something about it.

Accept the risk. When we accept a risk, we don't do anything further about it unless it occurs. If it occurs, we may take some remedial action, or we may simply absorb whatever it does to us.

Transfer the risk to someone else. Some risks aren't yours. They may belong to the customer, to someone higher up in the organization, or to someone with specific authority or expertise. You do have the responsibility for making sure that the correct risk owner is aware of the risk. You often need to follow up and monitor their risk responses.

Do something about the risk. For now, this means that we put the risk in a stack with other risks requiring action. Some risks are so urgent we need to move them to the head of the line and start working on them now. Others can wait until we start our risk response planning process, which follows risk analysis.

Category	Proposed Action	Intermediate Steps	Issues
Low Impact Risks	Accept unless response is easy and cheap	Review to make sure impact of risk is well understood and that nothing important is being overlooked	Linkages among risks may be overlooked; risks may change in impact based on other events
Low Probability Risks	If impact is moderate or less; accept unless response is easy and cheap	Review to make sure impact of risk is well understood and that nothing important is being overlooked	Linkages among risks may be overlooked; risks may change in likelihood based on other events

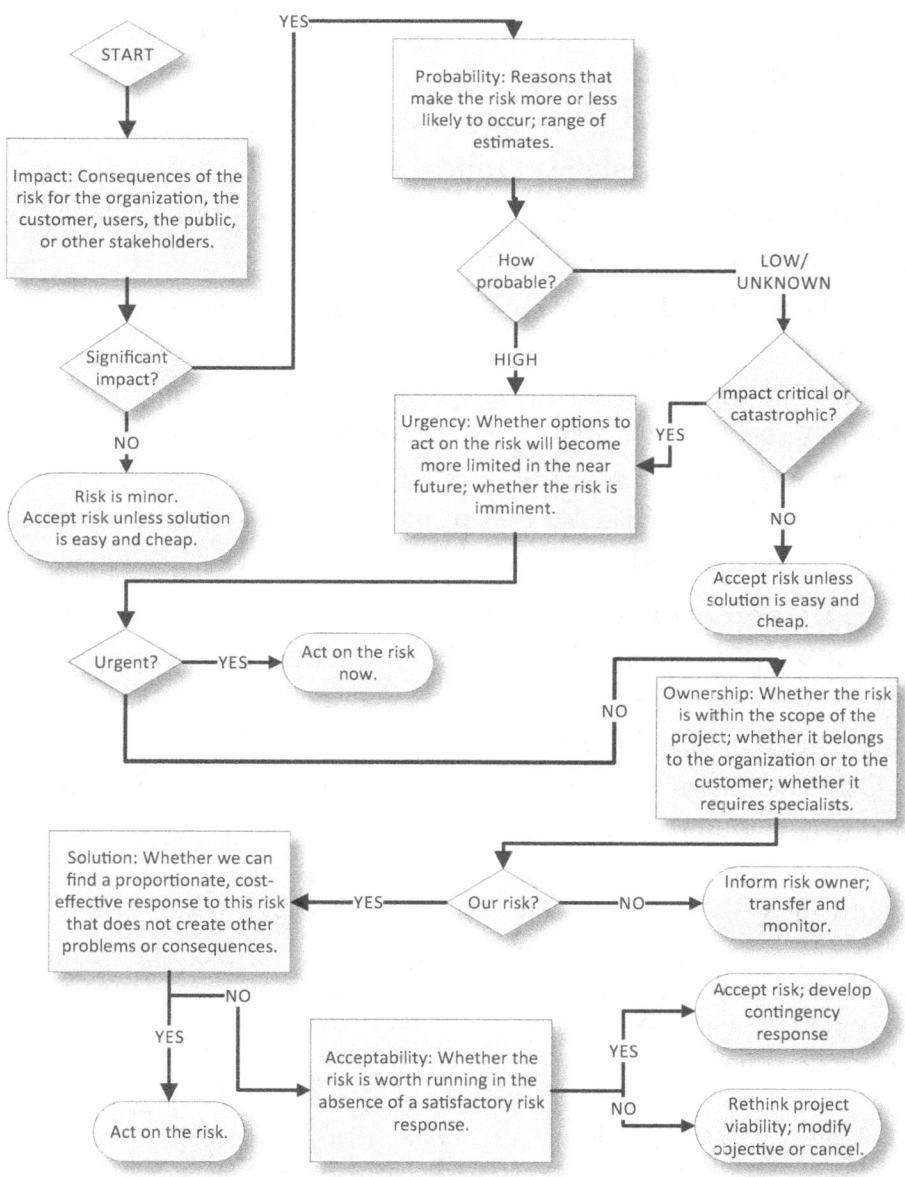

Urgent Risks	Start working on them as quickly as possible	Further information may be necessary to make a good decision	May draw attention from issues of potentially greater seriousness
Risks With Other Owners	Route risks to proper owners	Developing necessary information for risk owners	Defining proper ownership; ensuring risk owners take appropriate action
Risks Requiring Response	Develop and implement appropriate risk responses	Analyze risks to develop better understanding	Cost of response, levels of residual and secondary risk, opportunity costs
Serious Risks Without Effective Response	Decide whether the project can be changed; whether the risk is worth taking; whether the project is worth pursuing; contingency plans and recovery plans if the risk occurs	Further analysis data; identification of stakeholders and proper decision-makers; providing decision-makers with support	Impact of risk, secondary consequences of risk, cost of response

Fig 20. Risk Disposition Strategies

Risk Ranking

It's often the case that you have a general idea about probability, but there's no legitimate way for you to assign a firm number. You can rank risks into categories by using a risk ranking grid, shown in Figure 21.

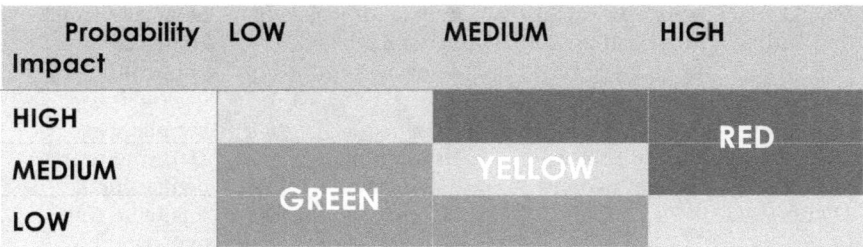

Fig 21. Risk Ranking Grid

Once you've decided whether probability and impact are high, medium, or low, just look where the columns intersect to find the ranking: red, yellow, or green. Deal with the red risks first, then yellow until you run out of resources or time. Deal with green risks when the solution is easy and cheap.

Risk Response Planning

Taking your prioritized list of risks, you now must come up with a potential strategy or solution for each. Depending on available resources and options, there may be a finite limit as to how much of the list you'll be able to treat. There are different options for negative risks (*threats*) and positive risks (*opportunities*). Two strategies work on any kind of risk.

Threat Responses

- **Avoidance.** Modify the project plan or strategy to remove the root cause of a risk. You can eliminate either the probability or the impact in avoiding the risk.

- **Mitigation.** Reduce the either the probability or the impact of the risk. There is still a risk and still project consequences of the risk, but the score is reduced.

- **Transfer.** Make someone else responsible for the risk event, or at least some portions of it. Insurance is a common method of risk transfer. Contract forms also transfer risk. In a fixed-price type contract, the seller owns the financial risk of something going wrong. In a cost-plus type contract, the buyer takes on that risk.

Opportunity Responses

- **Exploitation.** If you find an opportunity, you could take it. You've made an investment and it's increased in value. You sell the investment and take the money. Note that if the value of the investment continues to increase, you don't benefit.

- **Enhancement.** Don't take the benefit immediately, but adopt a strategy that increases either the probability or the impact of the potential gain.

- **Share.** If you're not the best person to take advantage of the opportunity, instead of letting it go to waste, give it to someone else.You might get something in return, but at a minimum there's good will.

For Either Kind of Risk

- **Contingent Response.** In most cases, if you adopt a risk response, you pay for it whether or not the risk event occurs. If you rent a tent because there's a risk it may rain on your picnic, you've paid for the tent even if it turns out to be a bright, sunny day. In a contingent response, you don't take the action unless the risk is *triggered*. For example, we check with the tent vendor and discover we can rent the tent as late as Thursday before the picnic. We check the weather forecast at noon on Thursday (the trigger), and make the decision then. (Note that for every contingent response you need to have a trigger, which can either be knowledge the risk event is about to occur or the opportunity to act is about to expire.

- **Acceptance.** Of course, you can always just accept the risk and do nothing at all. You might do this because the probability is exceedingly low or the impact is insignificant, or because the cost of any potential solution is wildly disproportionate to the value of the risk itself.

Update the risk register

Add analysis results and responses to the risk register. From time to time during the project, it's a good idea to review the risk register in case things have changed.

Modifying the plan for risk

Each risk response usually involves one or more *actions* that need to be taken. Those actions need to go into the active project schedule. Sometimes they are new activities ("Rent tent"); other times they modify requirements or strategies, or modify cost or duration.

In the case of *contingent responses*, add the trigger event to your schedule in the form of a milestone so people remember that the contingent action needs to be taken.

Contingency reserve

For risks that are accepted, or risks you aren't yet aware of, it's often a good practice to set aside a reserve. A *contingency reserve* or *contingency allowance* is normally in the form of extra money, but it can also be extra time or optional scope.

Risk Management and Control

Implementing the risk response plan. As with other elements of the planning process, you should end up with a written document, in the form of a table or narrative as you choose, that describes your risk management plan for the project. If you do similar projects, you can use previous risk management plans to build a template. Over time, as your understanding of risk improves, the document will become increasingly valuable to you and the organization. Identify major risk action points in your project schedule. You would most often use a milestone to do so.

Schedule risk management meetings periodically through your project, probably not as often as project status meetings, but regularly. Set a standard agenda for these meetings that involves reviewing the current plan, determining whether circumstances or improved knowledge changes any of your risk response strategies, identifying risks that have decreased and increased as project results have come in, and identifying new risks that only now have become apparent.

Updating and maintaining the plan. Either you as the project manager, or a team member who has been designated risk manager for the project should be operationally responsible for the plan. Use version numbers for document control, and identify the list of those who need current risk information—these likely include team members, the customer, and the project sponsor, and may include other important stakeholders.

Keep a record of decisions and alterations made as a result of your periodic risk review meetings. Prepare an archival report on risks and surprises for the project Lessons Learned file at the end.

Managing residual risks. Residual risks are risks you decided to accept and the remaining part of risks you have mitigated. By definition, these should be fairly minor—unless, of course, you've made a mistake or some risks have turned out to be far more serious than you expected.

Serious or not, the noise level risks on your project do require some attention. Are you seeing slippage on the critical path, budget creep, or tasks with lower quality outputs than expected? Day-to-day project adjustment is not unusual, and that becomes one more of your responsibilities as the project manager.

At the project's end, review the residual risk issue. Were the risks indeed residual, or were some more serious than you expected? Were there triggering factors or special circumstances that you would expect again? What would you do differently given the experience you just had?

Budgeting and Cost Estimating

The financial management of your project is usually important not only to you as a project manager, but also to others in your organization. It's not unusual to spend more time justifying the budget than presenting almost any other aspect of your project.

Your individual organization drives a significant portion of this project according to its own rules and procedures, and project managers do well when they take the time to learn those rules and work within them.

In business, it may surprise you to know that it's actually unusual for the cost constraint to be the Driver of the project. The reason is that most projects are undertaken because the perceived benefit significantly outweighs the cost. If that's the case, then going over budget is usually a better choice than failing to complete the project in a manner that delivers the benefit. However, expenditures in the present are easier to see than potential benefits in the future, so the emphasis on cost control is normally greater in practice than the underlying project dynamics would suggest.

Escalating the Cost Constraint

Because of the central nature of finance in business processes, it's normal that the problems in getting a budget and expending money on your project are numerous. From fiscal limits to political tensions, from operational issues to the overall economic environment, financial pressures and issues can be enormous.

Why are money matters so difficult?

People issues. First, people have a stake in money decisions, because every dollar on your project comes from somebody and goes to somebody. This naturally influences money matters, from the price a vendor charges to the size of the budget your manager allows. What's good for the project is only a single variable among many.

Risk issues. Second, projects have risk. It may be true that your project, if completed successfully, will earn us a million dollars. It would seem, therefore, that as long as you spend less than a million dollars in accomplishing the project, there's a profit. But that assumes that you successfully complete the project and that it performs to expectations and forecasts. How likely is that? If there's a 50-50 chance the market will embrace the project, then the expected value is only 50% x $1 million, or $500,000. Expect the organization to want to keep your budget more in line with the expected value, or even less.

Visibility issues. Third, lost money shows up more clearly on the bookkeeper's sheet than the cash value of a missed opportunity. If we pass up the opportunity to go for the million dollar project, that doesn't show up on the books as a loss. But if we spend $100,000 and have nothing to show for it, that's extremely visible, and could be damaging to our career prospects. There's a saying that "what gets measured gets performed." Sometimes the measurement issue militates against even worthwhile risk.

Control/hierarchy issues. Fourth, control of money is one of the central defining characteristics of management. Surrendering control of money is surrendering control, period. And not everyone is happy about surrendering control. Keeping rein on the purse strings is a way to keep control of the project.

Empty pockets. Finally, sometimes the money just isn't there, or is committed to other worthwhile projects. It's not that someone doesn't want to give you the resources you need, it's that they can't.

Strategies for Managing Budget Politics

Now that we see the problem, what about a solution? Here are some ideas.

Remember, no matter how effective you become, there's no guarantee that the project budget will come out the way you want. However, there are ways to increase the odds in your favor.

Learn the system and the context. Who controls the purse strings? What policies, procedures, and histories influence their decisions? Who else is competing for the money you need? Understanding the dynamic that surrounds you is an important tool.

Be honest about your own weaknesses. When we're trying to sell our project and our budget, we often emphasize the strong parts and deemphasize any areas of perceived weakness or vulnerability. That isn't necessarily the best strategy, because the managers reviewing your project can tell they're being sold. Instead, go through the project as they see it, addressing weaknesses and vulnerabilities in your own approach. Oddly, you'll find in most cases you're perceived better— not overoptimistic, not intending to pull the wool over management's eyes.

Avoid padding. Of course, padding is the traditional answer to perceived arbitrary management budget cutting. If they always chop your budget by 20 percent, it seems obvious that if you pad your budget by 20 percent, you'll end up okay. And it does work, for a while—until management figures out the game and starts cutting 40 percent. This way lies madness.

Although padding is a bad strategy, there are legitimate ways to achieve much the same goal. Develop a risk contingency plan that shows the extra costs of coping with specific events. Why aren't these the same as padding? Because you don't have to keep them secret. The costs show up clearly in your planning documents.

Develop allies. If you're up against someone in senior management who chooses to take an irrational view about your budget, the only response is to find another manager of equivalent (or higher) rank to work on your behalf. Start with your project sponsor, and work from there. Provide good staff support to your champion; make sure he or she has the figures and the facts.

Adjust the rest of the project. If cost becomes the Driver, then it follows that another constraint must be Weak. To manage the project within acceptable costs, you may have to make adjustments in the other constraints. Make sure you show clearly and objectively that you've tried to accommodate the cost pressures into your project with minimum compromise, but show the compromises you have to take.

Activity-Based Costing in Project Management

Each direct cost on a project occurs within an activity, or task. If there is a charge for labor, it's labor on a task. If you purchase equipment and supplies, it's part of a task. By assigning costs based on the activities in your project, you end up with a budget that reflects the course of the work of the project, making it easier to track and measure variance.

Your organization may look for other types of cost groupings, based on how it organizes and tracks its own expenditures. This is one reason why the second level of your WBS (blocks that have breakdown below them) is sometimes known as the control account level. In developing a WBS, you can establish the cost accounts as headers, and then classify each task under the cost account most suitable for it. Of course, tasks by their nature often cut across any set of categories you might set up. Therefore, expect that forcing tasks into cost accounts will lead to some borderline fits.

You might be expected to group costs by categories such as labor, materials, and services. In this sort of costing, each task is likely to have elements in each category. This may fit the organization's accounting needs better, but makes it much more difficult for you as a project manager to track costs and identify variances. Although you must, of course, do what the organization wants, you may find it useful to create your own activity-based costing linked to your own WBS for the purposes of internal tracking and monitoring.

Types of Project Costs

There are a number of different types of costs, each with special characteristics, that can affect the management and internal operations of your projects.

Direct Costs are those costs that can be specifically identified with a particular project, program, or activity. They include such things as the actual cost of labor, materials, supplies, and outside services. It's usually possible to assign direct costs to tasks, which is useful for project tracking.

You aren't always charged directly for what could easily be considered direct costs. One example is the cost of using employee labor on your project. In many organizations, your direct project budget isn't charged for employee labor costs. You must only account for costs that involve the actual payment of funds to someone outside the organization. That isn't a good project management practice from the organization's point of view, because it pushes you to make decisions that aren't in the financial best interest of the organization. Notice that in this case, it's always cheaper for your project budget to do it in-house, even if it really isn't. Now, if you didn't make the rules, then all you're obligated to do is to follow them. It's still appropriate to inform your project sponsor what's going on.

Fixed Costs are those costs that must be paid regardless of the volume or level of the project; they do not vary with quantity. If you are making a new product, there are huge costs associated with getting the first one manufactured. Tooling, art costs, preproduction, setup—these costs can mount up quickly. Let's imagine that there are one million dollars in upfront fixed costs. If you make only one item, all these costs will have to be counted against that one item, meaning it will cost one million dollars plus the variable cost of manufacturing for one copy. But if you make a million, then only one dollar would have to be charged against each product. That's why it's often substantially cheaper on a per-unit basis to order larger quantities.

Variable Costs are those costs that change depending on the volume or level of the project, such as labor. Even though we don't have to pay for tooling for each additional item coming off the production line, there are still some costs involved. We need the material for each item, the press or production time for each item, the cost of assembling the parts, the cost of packaging and shipping. These are variable costs because they vary with the number of units produced. Let's imagine there are five dollars in variable costs in manufacturing each item. The cost for one item is $1,000,005. The cost-per-piece for 100,000 is now ($1,000,000 + (100,000 x $5))/100,000, or $1,500,000/100,000, or $15 apiece. But the cost-per-piece of one million is only $1+$5, or $6 apiece.

Indirect Costs/Overhead. What percentage of the office electric bill is properly charged to your project? Obviously, you consume lighting and power for your computer. But maybe the light shines on more than one cubicle, and the network is shared among many machines. It would be silly to try to figure out these costs in detail, yet they are real. We classify these as indirect costs, because they can't easily be apportioned among multiple projects. In many situations, indirect costs won't be charged against your project at all, because you don't control them. Management will work in general to keep overhead under control.

When overhead is billed against your project, it's often billed as a percentage. If you spend $1 million in actual costs and there is a 20 percent overhead, then the project charge is $1.2 million.

If your project is a grant or government contract, an allowable overhead rate is part of the contract, and your organization will probably pocket that money at the beginning, leaving you the remainder. If the total price of the contract (remember that price is not cost) is $1 million, and there is a 20 percent overhead, then you have only $800,000 to spend.

Creating the Cost Baseline

The cost estimate on a project represents your idea of what it will cost to do the project. The budget, on the other hand, is a request for actual funds or the statement of actual funds available. Ideally, the numbers are related, but not in all cases.

Your operational project budget is the sum of the task budgets plus any general overhead burdens placed on the project. That ends up being true no matter which way you go. Sometimes, you develop the project budget by developing activity budgets for each task and summing them by cost account category. Of course, it's not unheard of to hear back from management that your budget has been cut 35 percent. Operationally, this means that the 35 percent cut has to be taken out of individual tasks, and an across-the-board meat axe approach is likely to spell disaster. Try to resolve conflicts like this before you get started.

In the actual management of your project, known as the Execution phase, you will want to track actuals against the plan. To do this, you need a cost baseline. By breaking down the project in terms of tasks, and showing the associated costs for each task, you can track your cumulative performance and thus identify any variances. Significant variances will demand action on your part.

Chapter 4:
Managing Your Project

THE *EXECUTING* PROCESS GROUP CONTAINS ALL THE activities necessary to accomplish the work of the project. You assign project activities to team members, help the team work together effectively, manage and resolve problems, and coordinate with project stakeholders.

At the same time, you'll also be working on Controlling activities, which involve monitoring status of project work against baselines, managing risks and quality, and handling changes to the original project.

You're not completely finished with planning, even though you're now going about the business of getting the work accomplished. When a project involves a high level of unknowns, as is common in such areas as R&D and new product development, your initial plan may have gotten quite sketchy after the first few tasks, because the output of those tasks determines what will happen subsequently. As a result, you may find yourself continuing to develop and refine the plan by adding new information as you obtain it.

Executing the project is the part of project management that is most like regular management. You delegate work to team members, motivate them to perform well, lead the project in a specific direction, and build an environment that allows people to achieve their best results.

Building the Project Team

The project team consists of the people whose work you need to get the project done. The team normally consists of a few people who are in the project pretty much from start to finish, and others who have specific technical roles to play. Once the roles have been satisfied, those people normally leave the project team. The team members may or may not be people who report to you in a traditional supervisory sense; some team members may have higher organizational rank than you.

Intact and Part-Time Work Teams

The project team can be either an intact work team or part time. An intact work team consists of people who are on the project full time, start to finish. Because they have little or no outside responsibilities during the life of the project, their time and effort are largely controllable by the project manager.

On a part-time work team, members of the work team have other projects and work responsibilities, and work on the current project only on a part-time basis (with occasional spurts of full-time effort).

It's much easier to build teamwork in an intact work team than in a part-time work team. However, projects tend to be set up based on the practical nature of the work, not on the ideal circumstances for effective teamwork. Nevertheless, if you are the project manager, you must build a spirit of willing collaboration and cooperation or else the job is unlikely to be done, or done very well.

Teamwork in an Intact Work Team

Let's look at the easier situation first: building a team in an intact environment. First, the circumstances and nature of the work have to permit this choice. Second, you may or may not have significant power to choose the team members you prefer. Third, even if the majority of your team has an intact structure, it's common for at least some members to connect on a part-time basis.

Projects fail in the execution stage for three basic reasons:

- People on the team do not know the goals, the individual roles, or the performance expectations for the project
- People get bogged down in the act of working with one another because they do not possess the necessary skills
- Rivalries, politics, and personalities (and previous histories) generate conflict

Teamwork and team building is frequently misunderstood, and you may have seen it presented in what is essentially a set of feel-good activities. Teams are necessary in organizations because they are a critical tool to get the work done. As a project manager, you must understand fundamental team building techniques and strategies in order to get your projects accomplished, such as the following:

G-R-E-A-T Teamwork

The GREAT model specifies what each member of a project team must know before they can work together effectively.

GOALS. What are the goals of the project? What is the goal of each individual activity? Why are we doing this?

ROLES. What is my job as an individual team member? What do I do? What is the contribution that I am expected to make? What expertise do I bring to the situation? What is everyone else's role and everyone else's expected contribution?

EXPECTATIONS. How good is good enough? What is the level of performance that is desired? What level of performance is *not* desired? Why are the expectations set at this level as opposed to another?

ACCOUNTABILITIES/ABILITIES. Who is *accountable* for each phase of the work, especially on jobs that cut across functional lines or involve several people? What *abilities* do we possess that have a bearing on the individual job assignments?

TIMING. When must this be done? At what pace am I to work? How does the timing of one piece of the work affect other pieces?

Don't assume people know this or will figure it out on their own. Set a personal rule that you will deliver this information a minimum of three times: verbally to the group, in writing to the group, verbally to each individual, and in written form to each individual.

Other Skills

Working Together Skills. Some of the most important skills of working together are not systematically taught to people. To work together in a business setting, people must know how to run a meeting, how to conduct group decision-making and problem-solving, and other group processes.

Personality issues. A good team involves people who bring disparate personality styles and sets of strengths/weaknesses to the situation. Use personality type systems, such as the Myers-Brigs Type Indicator, to help each team member understand the others and understand that the goal is to get people to operate with mutual respect, rather than necessarily to like each other or even enjoy working with each other.

The Tuchman Model

Even when you do everything right, know that teams naturally pass through a set of stages known as the

Tuchman Model, illustrated in Figure 22. Each stage has predictable challenges. Don't mistake a natural developmental phase for an actual problem.

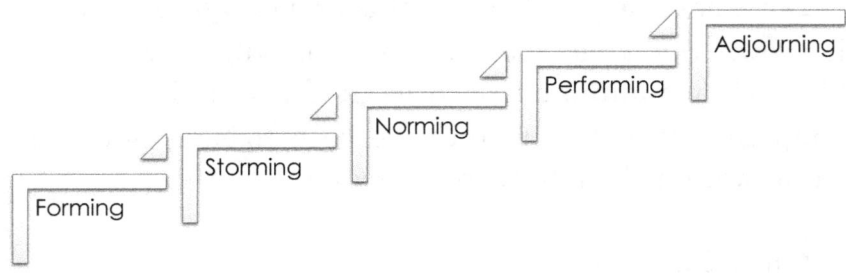

Fig 22. The Tuchman Model

The last stage, "Adjourning," is an addition for projects, which are temporary in nature. Shutting down and dismantling the team once the job is over can be more difficult and emotionally challenging than you think. There's research that suggests that most conflicts early in the project are about issues, not personalities (though personalities may well come into play). At the project end, oddly, emotional issues sometimes rise to the forefront, and conflicts often are about something other than actual issues.

Teamwork in a Part-Time Work Team

If all or some of the members of the team are not part of an intact work team structure, you still have to accomplish the same goals, but you have fewer tools to work with.

The GREAT model becomes even more important in this situation. When people have their attention divided among multiple projects, you simply cannot assume that they have enough focus on your project to know what the expectations are. Telling them verbally a single time just doesn't cut it. Do tell them, but write them, e-mail them, and put it in your calendar that you have to remind them when it comes to the timing issues. Your firm persistence is the most valuable tool you have.

Know that you will often have to settle for minimum performance from people because your project simply doesn't have a high enough priority, and if it does, it's still not an absolute priority.

The better your own skills at the disciplines of meeting management, conflict resolution, etc., the better you'll perform in this situation.

One common complaint of project managers in the part-time team environment is, "I schedule a meeting, but key players just don't show up!" That's because meetings have an unfortunately deserved reputation as time-wasters, and busy people will attempt to dodge them if possible. When you do them right, you'll find that in time the word gets around and people are much more likely to be cooperative.

If you are in the common position of having to aid other people on their projects while managing your own, make sure you provide support to others on a timely basis if you expect to have enough influence to push them into completing your work on time. Keep good calendar records and practice effective time management.

Supervising People Who Don't Work For You

It's very common for a project manager not to be the official supervisor of the entire project team. This is true because projects are temporary, requiring a variety of people to be pulled under one roof for a limited amount of time. Because they have homes to return to after the conclusion of the project, and because their expertise may be needed on a variety of projects, it makes little sense to reorganize the entire table of organization for this limited purpose.

The good news is that official supervisory authority isn't that great to begin with. While you may possess the technical power to fire somebody, in practice, you must get the cooperation and signoffs of people who outrank you in your own hierarchy and of outside groups (such as human resource or legal) to get it done. Supervisors quickly learn that official power is much less important than leadership—the ways we get people to choose to do what it is we want them to do.

The discipline of influence management, which is a practical and completely legitimate form of office politics, is another of the core competencies of good project managers.

Influence management is, as the name suggests, the art and craft of gaining influence over others, which requires power. There are six sources of organizational power that reinforce one another to give you expanded influence to get the work done.

Types of Power

Power, engineers tell us, is energy that overcomes resistance to achieve work. That's as true in organizational life as it is in the physical world. You need power to get anything done.

There are, of course, ethical issues in gaining and using power, but the fact that some people may handle power in unethical ways shouldn't scare us away from using it at all. It's perfectly possible — and clearly desirable — to be both ethical and effective. The "smart thing" and the "right thing" are very often the same thing, especially when you take a long-term perspective.

Figure 23 shows the six types of formal power.

ROLE Power. Your official role in the organization, along with special delegated assignments, committee and staff positions, etc., gives you certain influence. Even those who do not report to you in a formal sense normally have to show at least a minimum respect for your organizational role. Notice that this power is given to you by others, and is capable of being countermanded.

RESPECT Power. A powerful source of influence management is the respect others have for you, because of your track record, your special knowledge, your insight and intelligence, and your personal integrity and honesty. While respect power takes time to build, it's often much more powerful than organizational role in influencing the behavior of others.

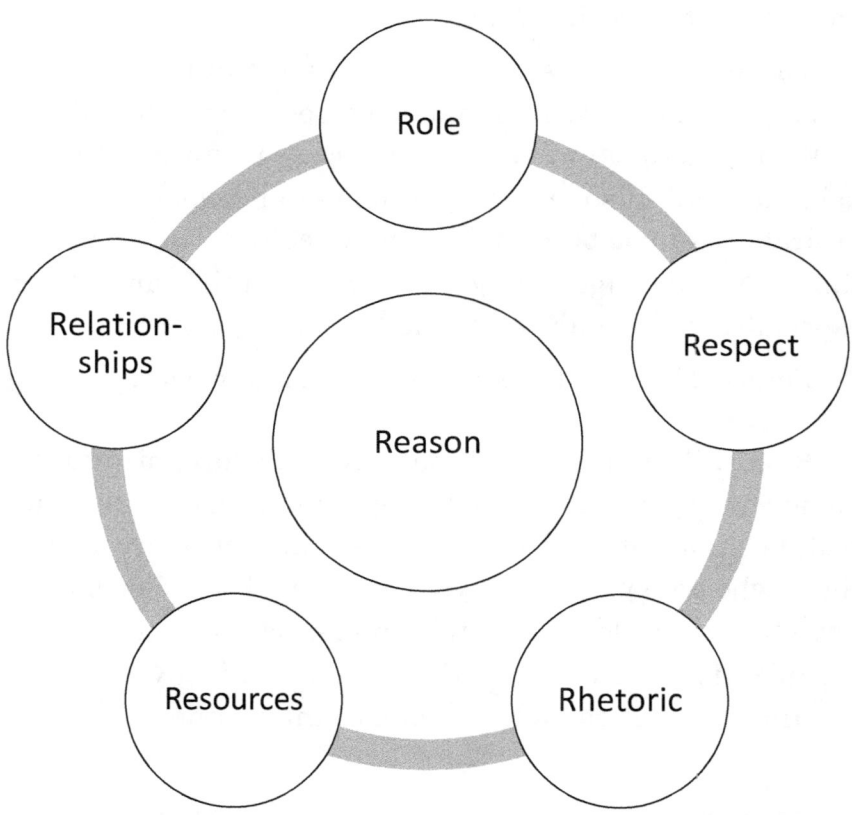

Fig 23. The POWER Model

RHETORIC Power. Skill in the arts of communication is a source of influence and power. A clearly written memo setting forth goals, roles, expectations, and time requirements for a specific task is harder to ignore than a badly written and confusing one. Your personal ability to negotiate, to sell, and sometimes even to plead are ways to influence others to get the work done.

RESOURCES Power. You often have control of certain resources—your own time and priority list, if nothing else—that others require to get their work done. While it's in the long run ineffective to try to deny others to blackmail them into cooperating with you, it's legitimate to go the extra mile for those who are willing to go the extra mile for you in return.

RELATIONSHIP Power. Who you know and what kind of relationship you have with them is another traditional source of power. Some people interpret this too narrowly, and only suck up. But notice the power held by someone who has a staff-level friend in every department. Good manners and a friendly smile are effective influence management tools available to anyone.

REASON Power. Depending on the priority of your project, you may get additional power from it. Reason power comes from the "Why?" of your project. Under normal circumstances, you couldn't evict a vice president from his or her office, but if you're the acting fire marshal and there's a fire, your reason for giving orders is so high that everyone will tend to obey you. Faking a higher level of priority for your project is normally a bad idea, but when your project has significant priority and legitimacy, it's completely appropriate to use that power in support of accomplishing your ends.

Managing Tasks and Deliverables

While managing your team processes, you must ensure that the right tasks are completed in the right order. Give work assignments in writing, and keep a log. Follow up at regular intervals. Insist that people tell you when they're completed in writing—it keeps them focused. You'll find that your WBS, network diagram, Gantt chart, and other traditional project management tools help you do this.

Don't forget to involve your customer in the process. If you complete some project deliverables before the project is completed, turn them over early and get written confirmation that they are acceptable—it puts you in good shape with the customer and adds to the customer's confidence in your performance as a project manager.

Keeping On Schedule, On Budget, and On Spec

There is a feedback loop between the project phases of Execution and Controlling. By staying on top of the team process and ensuring that task assignments are given and received in written form, you are providing operational emphasis on the three project management goals: on time, on budget, and on spec.

Of course, there are reasons other than poor performance that result in missed deadlines, budgets, or performance targets. Perhaps the job had a high degree of inherent uncertainty, so the original estimate wasn't that solid. Perhaps unforeseen and even unforeseeable problems cropped up. Perhaps outside priorities interfered with your planned acquisition and utilization of project resources.

Whatever the reason, your monitoring and control systems will need to pick them up. Based on your analysis, you will then make performance changes that normally require work in the Execution phase, and so you can expect a steady stream of adjustments and modifications.

Project Control

The other major activity of the project manager once the project has started is *Controlling* the project. In the Controlling phase, your mission is to monitor the project as compared to the original plan, and to act to correct deviations, and to manage the scope of the project, including handling required project changes.

While the Executing process is mostly involved with the members of your team, the Controlling process tends to involve people outside your team—stakeholders, customers, managers, contractors—who have their own agendas and interests concerning your project. You'll find yourself using substantial negotiating skills during this phase as well.

How do you know how you're doing? By examining actual data compared to performance baselines.

Setting Up Performance Baselines

There are normally three performance baselines that you set for your project: the schedule baseline, the cost baseline, and the technical baseline.

Schedule baseline. The first baseline is the *schedule,* normally displayed in the form of a Tracking Gantt Chart. On a Tracking Gantt Chart, you have one set of bars that represent the original plan, and a parallel set that record what has already happened on the project. By comparing the two, you can identify schedule discrepancies and identify their potential impact on the project.

Cost baseline. The second performance baseline is the cost baseline. There isn't a standard tool like the Tracking Gantt to display this information. Normally, you'll use a spreadsheet showing the budget amounts for each task, enter the actual cost when it's determined, and monitor the variance, if any.

Technical baseline. The third baseline is the technical baseline, which normally involves monitoring of the tasks displayed in your WBS to ensure that each is satisfactorily completed.

By recording when each activity is completed, you can monitor performance by department, which is a different and often useful perspective, especially on large projects with numerous tasks. You can compare completion dates with targets, but the scheduling baseline has already given you that information.

What you want to look at is the project from the perspective of work complete, and in this view you can also see any patterns that are developing within departments or subprojects in time to allow you to act.

Managing Risks

As we've said before, there are four parts to an overall risk management strategy, and they start in the planning stage of your project. These are risk identification, risk quantification, risk response planning, and risk response control. Throughout your project you will find it wise to periodically reassess the probability of the risks you've identified because events on your project make some risks likelier or less likely. You can then amend your planning and response to deal with them.

Maintaining Quality

Quality and performance are not synonymous. Quality is what you want; performance is what you do. If you want performance on your project to be quality, that takes effort in Planning, Execution, and Control. Quality is never an accident, but a result of deliberate action, and the project manager is operationally responsible for quality.

Defining Quality

If quality is not defined, or thought of as some vague concept of "goodness," you can't very well pursue it methodically. In the discipline of Total Quality

Management (TQM), there are several schools of thought, each with their own definition.

One well-known definition comes from W. Edwards Deming, who defined quality as "exceeding customer expectations." The value in this definition is that it relates to the behavior we are seeking. If a customer is dissatisfied, the customer goes somewhere else next time. If a customer is satisfied, but no more, he or she may seek a lower price or try someone else just to see what's out there. But if a customer has his or her expectations exceeded, then the customer will come back, and usually price is not the primary purchasing consideration.

The limit of this definition is that the project manager or project team doesn't always have direct access to the customer. If you don't know what the customer expectations happen to be, it's rather difficult to plan to exceed them.

Another popular definition of quality comes from the work of Philip Crosby, who defines quality as "conformance to requirements." Let's define precisely what you want, then we will deliver it precisely as you requested.

The advantage of this definition is that operationally the project team is in a much better position to plan to achieve the requirements. The limit is that now you are the hostage of the person who specified the requirements. If that person didn't do a good job of working with the customer to develop the right requirements, you'll accurately deliver the wrong thing. And even though in one sense it isn't your fault—after all, you did what you were told—the negative customer consequences tend to fall on your head regardless of actual fault.

My own favorite definition of quality comes from President Bill Clinton, who once said, "It ain't dog food if the dog don't eat it." That's a good way to distinguish real quality from gold plating. To call something quality, it has to offer a meaningful benefit to a meaningful stakeholder. If it doesn't, it's gold plating. While quality is a good thing, gold plating is usually a waste.

Ideally, you want to work with multiple definitions in a feedback loop. The focus on the customer tells you with whom you must work, and a set of measurable, definable requirements you can integrate into your project is the output.

Look for opportunities to measure and test; you don't want a quality definition based on someone else's intuitive sense of whether what you've done is "good enough." That being said, even if you don't plan to settle for "good enough," it's an important baseline. You need to know where good enough lives in order to do better.

Operational Quality

We've emphasized elsewhere the importance of defining good enough, and that's not in opposition to quality. Both time and cost matter to customers, and in some circumstances trump the performance. If you're bleeding in the emergency room, you don't want to hear, "If you can wait until Tuesday, we can give you much finer quality." Adequate performance immediately is more valuable than technically superior performance several days later after you've already bled to death. Sometimes the use to which the customer will put a product is limited. An inexpensive product that does just enough is more desirable than a more expensive one full of bells and whistles of marginal value.

If your project runs into trouble, what should you cut? You can miss the deadline, exceed the budget, or aim lower on the performance requirements—the critical question is which does least damage to the customer's core needs? Good enough matters.

In your risk plan, consider risks to quality along with risks to schedule and budget. What could happen in this project that would lower our ability to deliver a quality product? Could we modify the project to lower either the probability or impact of the potential obstacles to quality?

If we have extra time or extra budget available, is it better to speed up the project or lower its cost, or is it better to invest any extra time, money, or resources in improving the performance? Answers vary from project to project.

If you begin your project with a focus on quality, and build quality measurements into your planning process, you will have operational control of quality throughout the project execution phase. It's worth doing.

Change Management

Even with good will on the part of all project stakeholders, projects, as we've learned, have a tendency to mutate. *Change management* is one of the critical functions of the Controlling process group. Changes can result from plan slippage in the areas of schedule, budget, resources, or performance; from the discovery of previously unknown information during the Execution of the project, or because one or more stakeholders wants something different now that the project has begun.

Preventive Action

The first category of project changes involves preventive action. Preventive action is taken with the goal of avoiding a problem by changing something in the way the project is managed. This could involve adding time to an activity, adding resources or money, or changing some aspect of performance or method. Preventive action can be designed into an initial plan, or be added to a project underway based on your ongoing risk identification.

Corrective Action

Corrective action is reactive: there has been a problem and the corrective action is designed to mitigate or eliminate the damage.

Scope Creep

A change in project scope can be part of either preventive or corrective action, but other changes in project scope aren't an indication of project problems. They are the result of a change requested by a project stakeholder, either the customer or someone else with an interest in the project. (Adding your objectives onto someone else's project is a traditional political technique, like attaching a rider to legislation already on the fast track.)

Scope creep isn't inherently wrong—it may be necessary, appropriate, even desirable—but it is troublesome, because changes in scope normally affect other parts of the project. If someone wants you to do additional work, it's likely to take additional time, cost additional money, take additional resources, or affect your ability to do another part of the project. Therefore, you need to manage project scope actively, and that's one of the key activities in the Controlling phase of your project.

Earlier, we identified that the Planning portion of our project must include an advance strategy for how we will deal with requested scope changes during the project. The strategy was 1) everything in writing, 2) assessed for impact, 3) presented to the decision maker (who may be the project manager or may not be), and 4) if approved, implemented—along with other changes to the project.

Beware of the temptation to be nice and shortcut the process. This tends to get you in later trouble, especially because people requesting a scope change tend to verbally minimize what they are really asking for. You want to make sure the entire change is quantified so that the decision-making process will be meaningful.

Change Management in Practice

One important decision to make with respect to scope changes is who pays for them. In construction projects, for example, the question of who is financially responsible for each change is a matter of careful contractual negotiation.

For each change, the question is whether it was within the original scope.

One problem seen in many organizations is that project managers (who may not be the sales or contract executive on the job) often feel embarrassed or unsure how to ask for additional money for out-of-scope change orders. They accept out-of-scope changes with the goal of customer goodwill.

It may sometimes be appropriate to eat costs that aren't really your responsibility based on the extent and nature of the customer relationship, but you don't get the goodwill if the customer doesn't know the sacrifice you're making. Provide a "zero cost" change order at a minimum, showing the price you would normally charge, and then waiving it. You may be glad later on that you have earned some goodwill with the customer, because later on you may have to use it.

Replanning

In some cases it is appropriate to reopen the planning process to deal with change. Because planning takes resources and time (and sometimes money), a comprehensive replanning of the project is not something lightly undertaken.

Consider replanning the project if the scope change is large, if you have to develop a new method to get from where you are back to where you want to be, and if mapping actual progress against your benchmarks no longer gives you information useful in decision-making.

Task Management

The fundamental purpose of project execution is to get the work done on time, on budget, and to the desired standard of performance. Everything else is a method or a technique to support that goal. Teamwork matters a lot, but remember that we have teams in the work environment because we need the work done.

An additional benefit of project management is that the structured tools for task management and control help you delegate, train, and coach, delivering not only a product at the end of the project, but also leaving team members with more skill than they had to begin with.

Negotiating Task Performance

Why would you have to negotiate task performance when you're the project manager? Should that not be expected? Unfortunately, as you've no doubt realized, your official authority and about $4 will get you a tall skim latte, extra shot—but that's about all.

Have you ever met an unmotivated person? The answer may seem obvious, but it's a trick question. Look at it this way: Have you ever met someone who spends more time dodging work than it would take to do it? Now, ask yourself, "Is this person unmotivated?" In fact, the person *is* motivated, but not in the direction you might want. Motivation is why someone is behaving in a particular way. If you don't like the behavior, a good strategy is to start by determining the motivation.

Basically, there are only three reasons why someone isn't doing what you want. They don't know, they can't do it, or they're making a choice—they *won't* do it. How you approach the issue depends on what's going in.

No matter how important your job assignment happens to be, it's almost never the only thing on someone else's agenda. When that person looks at your request, it naturally gets compared to the other demands, and it's not necessarily true that yours will win.

How, then, can you negotiate? Once you know the potential problem issue on the other side, you're in a position where you have the opportunity to negotiate. If you can solve their problem, there's a good chance they'll help solve yours.

Another way to look at this is to realize that you do favors for colleagues that you aren't actually required to do. Why do you do them? It may be because they've helped you (or may in the future), because they asked nicely, because you understood why their request was important, because you're a team player, or a host of other reasons (including negative ones, such as difficulty saying "no"). The motivations of others and your own motivations probably won't synch one hundred percent of the time, but usually at least some of what works on you will work on others, too.

The Task Management Form

One of the fundamentals of getting people to do things is to give them clear and complete information on exactly what you want. You've probably had the experience of trying to do what you heard someone say only to find out at the end that it wasn't what that someone actually wanted. In the absence of a tape recorder, we can't always be sure whether they said it badly or we heard it badly, but the outcome is the same. If you want others to do work for you and do it correctly, it's up to you to take the steps necessary to ensure understanding.

A powerful and effective tool is the Task Management Form. This form provides a home for all the information you need to understand what's involved in a particular task, and is therefore a very effective way to delegate. Properly done, it tends to eliminate "don't know" type difficulties with tasks.

If you've got a fairly large project, completing a Task Management Form for each activity can be time consuming. To reduce the time involved, consider these strategies: (1) Have the team members who will do the task do most of the work of preparing the form. This also achieves improved buy-in and identifies potential problems early. (2) Recycle Task Management Forms from previous projects with similar activities. Remember that templates don't always go down perfectly; expect to edit the information.

Completing the Task Management Form

While you're welcome to use this form for your own projects, you're normally better off adapting it. There may be too much fine detail in some areas and not enough in others, depending on your organization and the nature of your project. Form design and development is a

Chapter 4: Managing Your Project | 163

surprisingly sophisticated activity, and a really well-done form can make a significant difference in your results.

Figure 24 gives you a basic form for this purpose. Most of the fields are self-evident, and most use information you've already developed in your planning process. Here are a few additional notes.

[Project Name]	[Version/Date]
Activity/WBS No:	Activity Name:
Predecessor Task(s):	Successor Task(s):
Specifications/Deliverables:	
Resources—People/Department:	Resources—Other:
Time Estimate:	Cost Estimate:
Milestones/Dates:	

Assigned To: _____ Date Assigned :_____

Fig 24. Activity Management Form

Task Name: Make sure the name actually gives a sense of the work. One good practice is to think of a task as an action, described with a verb followed by a noun.

Predecessor/Successor Task(s): This information helps the person assigned the task to understand the consequences of being late.

Specifications/Deliverables: Deliverables are the physical outputs of the task. Specifications involve the measurable characteristics of the task

Resources: The form has spaces for people as well as tools/equipment.

Time Estimate: You may fill in a single time or date, or you may need to complete more information. If there's an imposed date situation, you need to write down the date itself, the type (fixed early start, finish no later than, etc.), and the reason. If you omit the reason, you may omit the motivation to achieve the date.

Milestones show the completion of parts of the task, and help measure progress. They also help you manage people of lower work maturity—more milestones gives you better control.

Cost Estimate: The cost estimate may have numerous elements. Use those appropriate to your own organization.

Assigned to/Date: It's also a good idea to note the date of completion as well as any specific milestones.

Kanban Task Management

There are immediate virtues and benefits in using a Task Management Form system. You can increase the benefit by using a *kanban* task management technique.

In the late 1940s, Taiichi Ohno, an engineer (later executive vice president) of Toyota Motor Company, had a leadership role in development of the innovative and influential Toyota Production System. One element of the system was just-in-time (JIT) inventory, using a system called *kanban*, a Japanese term referring to printed cards. When you needed new parts and supplies for your line, you would "purchase" them using *kaban* cards for your own line, triggering reorders up the system. Our kaban system does not use cards, but the term is chosen with a "thanks and a tip o' the hat" to Taiichi Ohno.

Step 1. Create a project binder that contains all the documents and printouts that your project generates. Put some notebook paper in it so that every handwritten note or meeting minute is kept together. In your project binder, put *two* copies of every Task Management Form.

Step 2. To assign a task on your project, give one copy of the Task Management Form for that activity to the person you assign. Write that person's name in the "Assigned To" space, and the date on which the work was assigned. The person who received the assignment is now accountable for it.

Step 3. During regular status meetings and other project control activities, make notes about progress on the activity on your copy of the Task Management Form. Use notebook paper placed after the form as necessary. Keep all information about the task together in your binder.

Step 4. The person performing the task is also responsible for reporting status. There are two types of status reports: *regular* reports that occur on the time schedule in conjunction with status reviews, and *special* (also known as *exception)* reports, which identify any unusual issues or problems experienced in doing the work.

Step 5. Problems identified in exception reports and change orders generated by the project generate special meetings with the project manager to resolve problems as they occur. If necessary, the task information is modified. Both project manager and task manager initial any changes and report the dates of those changes.

Step 6. The person assigned the task completes the task in line with any approved changes, verifies with checkmarks that all deliverables and specifications have been achieved, and signs the Task Management Form certifying that the task has been completed.

Step 7. The task is only considered officially complete when the signed Task Management Form is returned to the project manager.

Step 8. The Task Management Form, any notes, changes, and history become part of the paper trail of the project that is reviewed during project evaluation and Lessons Learned.

You'll find with this system that people's attitudes toward the work change when the documentation and control changes. A traditional management maxim has it that "what gets measured, gets done," and this method helps ensure your tasks get the focus they require.

Supporting vs. Controlling

You need to get clear in your own mind for the specific project how much emphasis you need to put on the on-the-job training portion of your responsibility. If people need to learn how to do these tasks because they will need to do them on a fairly regular basis, giving people the opportunity to flounder around a little as they learn the job is in the long-term best interest of the organization, if not completely in the best interest of the project.

If the project is high priority and on an unbendable deadline, you might need to compromise the goal of helping people learn and turn your attention instead to how to get it done quickly and correctly, even if that violates generally applicable principles of delegation.

And, if the project is so far outside the normal responsibilities of your team members that it's highly unlikely they'll need to master the skills involved, you may also choose a more active management strategy.

Don't wing this. Make up your mind at the beginning of the project what circumstances demand, tell your team members to get their expectations in the right place, and be consistent. It's often tempting to start interfering as soon as the first sign of storm clouds appear on the horizon, but if people don't work through a tempest or two, they aren't really able to learn very much.

Ensuring Quality Performance

People not only have to do the job, but do it well. Our earlier focus on quality planning comes back to the forefront in task management. We should already know what quality means on each specific activity and for the project as a whole. To achieve quality goals, first make sure the information is shared with the people who do the work. If they don't know the quality goals, it's highly unlikely they'll be motivated to meet them.

Second, implement measurement. While one value of measurement is that it identifies variance (especially special cause variance) in time for you to act on it, another value of measurement is that it is feedback to the person performing the task. The second value is more in line with an overall commitment to progress. We identify variance not so we can come in and punish the offenders, but so the workers can learn early that there is a potential problem and solve it before the baby monster turns into a full-grown Godzilla.

Third, keep team members focused on the customer and the project goal. It's difficult sometimes for people in the trenches to see the big picture, and sometimes the big picture slips out of view altogether. One of your key quality objectives as project manager is to ensure that people not only know *what* they're doing, but also *why* they're doing it.

Don't forget to keep your own focus clear. There's an old cartoon with the caption "When you're up to your rear end in alligators, it's hard to remember that your original objective was to drain the swamp." That's literally true— it is hard to remember, especially under stress and in the middle of a crisis. But remember you must keep focused, especially when it becomes most difficult. Your focus is a central part of your ability to keep the project on track, and deliver the goods—alligators or not.

Baselines and the Tracking Gantt Chart

In our projects, it's valuable to establish baselines— measurable elements of the project against which we can set actual performance, with the goal of determining how big and potentially how meaningful each variance we discover is.

The Importance of Baselines

In planning your project, we've recommended that you develop detailed schedules, budgets, and technical plans to ensure that you fully understand your own project. The payoff you get from the planning work just in those terms is normally enough to make it worth your while, but there's more value to extract. Your planning documents, once complete and accepted, become the foundation for your project tracking and monitoring system by turning into baselines.

If you want to make sure your project is on time, on budget, and to spec, you want to be able to measure your progress on those three axes. There are three primary project baselines you need to manage your project, corresponding to the Triple Constraints. The first is the *schedule baseline,* which is normally presented as a Tracking Gantt Chart. The second is the cost baseline, a cumulative graph showing actual vs. planned expenditures to date. And the third is the technical baseline (also called the performance baseline), which is often linked to the WBS.

Using the Technical Baseline for Deliverables and Requirements

You developed the WBS to ensure that you described the scope and the deliverables in terms of tasks and activities necessary to complete them. You can use the same tool as a technical baseline to ensure good performance. If you've adopted our Activity Management Form approach, it can easily work as a technical baseline.

Cost Baselines and Financial Management

There are a variety of styles for presenting your cost baseline, as well. The cost baseline comes from the final approved project budget, and takes the total amount available to spend and allocates those expenditures for individual activities. Depending on how you're expected to break down and report costs, such things as overhead rates may be applied against the total budget. In that case, your operating budget is your total budget less indirect cost charges. You must allocate your operating budget, not the total budget, to the tasks in your project in constructing the cost baseline, because it's the operating expenditures that you need to measure.

It's perfectly legitimate to display the information in a spreadsheet form. If you start using the Earned Value Method (see below) a spreadsheet is virtually required. In addition, cost baselines (and some Earned Value measures) work very well in graph form.

Earned Value Project Management

The Earned Value method of project management is an advanced tool available for you as a project manager. Most often used in the construction industry, Earned Value offers a powerful set of analytical and forecasting tools to measure, monitor, and predict cost and schedule variance. It starts with three measurements:

The **Planned Value (PV)** of the project is how much the plan says you should have spent to achieve the work that should have been done by a given date.

The **Actual Cost (AC)** of the project is how much you have spent by a given date to accomplish the work you actually did by that date, whether or not it's the same as the work you planned to get done.

The **Earned Value (EV)** of the project is how much you should have spent to accomplish the work you actually got done by a given data. Think of it in terms of a progress payment: you only get paid for the work you got done, and you get paid what was agreed to for that work.

Various formulae based on these three items provide you with extensive tools to analyze your performance. Here are a few of the more popular tools:

Schedule Variance (SV) = PV – EV. How much work did we get done based on how much we planned? If we should have completed $1,000 worth of work by today but have only done $800, we're $200 behind schedule.

Cost Variance (CV) = EV – AC. In accomplishing $800 worth of work, we may have spent $900. In that case, we're also $100 over budget.

Schedule Performance Index (SPI) = EV/PV. How are we doing against the schedule? If we've done $800 worth of work when we should have done $1,000, then our SPI is 80 percent. We're running 20 percent behind schedule.

Cost Performance Index (CPI) = EV/AC. If we've spent $900 to do $800 worth of work, then our CPI is 89 percent. We're running 11 percent over budget.

The power of the Earned Value as a forecaster can be easily seen. If we've completed 20 percent of a $500,000 project and have an SPI of 80 percent and a CPI of 89 percent, that's a disturbing trend. The estimated final cost of this project (EAC, or Estimate at Completion) is determined by taking the total budget (BAC, or Budget at Completion) and dividing it by the CPI.

$$EAC = BAC/CPI = \$500,000 / 89\% = \$561,797$$

According to the Earned Value model, it looks like we'll be a little more than $60,000, or around 12% over budget.

Tracking Gantt Chart

The schedule baseline returns us to the Gantt Chart. The big advantage of a Tracking Gantt Chart prepared by software is that it will automatically project the effect of schedule variances out to the end of the project. Making a Tracking Gantt is easy. Take the original project Gantt chart and add a second bar to each activity (Figure 25). The bottom bar is the original schedule; the top bar is actual completion (if done) or forecast actual completion. (Software can do this automatically.) A quick look at a Tracking Gantt can tell you if you're on track or slipping.

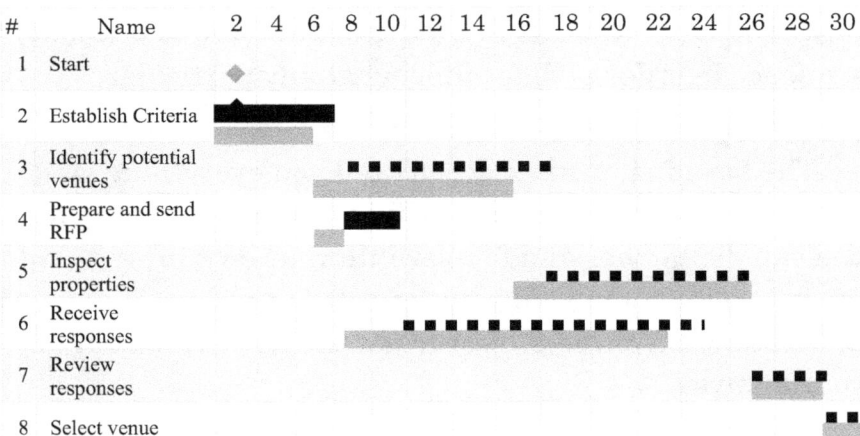

Fig 25. Tracking Gantt Chart

Interpreting a Tracking Gantt Chart

In Figure 25, Activity 2 "Establish Criteria" took a day longer than planned, and its successor Activity 3 "Prepare and send RFP" both started late and took longer.

However, as we remember, Activity 3 isn't critical, so we have the potential to recover. The dotted lines on the Tracking Gantt are forecasts based on actuals-to-date. Notice that while Activity 5 "Inspect Properties" is forecast to start late, it finishes on time. This suggests we've either chosen to visit fewer sites or sent out more than one team; either way, we will be able to recover the project and forecast finishing on time.

The mere fact that an actual bar is longer than a plan bar doesn't automatically mean that you have a schedule problem. As you remember, a delay in a critical task automatically creates a delay in the project's end date, but a delay in a noncritical task only affects the project end date if it's greater than the available slack or float for that task. You have to know your critical path and dependency sequence in order to determine what any particular variance means or doesn't mean.

The baseline by itself doesn't tell you everything you need to know. It serves as a picture and a tool by which you can dig farther and farther into your own project. You must normally apply all your knowledge and understanding of the project to get the most value out of your analysis.

When to Replan and Rebaseline Your Project

There are three basic situations that make you think about replanning and rebaselining a project. These are imposed changes/scope creep, internal changes/variances, and circumstantial/environmental changes.

Imposed changes/scope creep. The baseline of the project consists of the approved original plan plus or minus approved changes. When you have scope creep, your baseline gets modified. If the changes are relatively minor, you may not bother to update your baseline information. You can simply eyeball the baseline and interpret what it means.

If the changes are more significant, it will likely be advantageous for you to generate updated plans and new baselines. Another advantage of computer tools in project management is that automation is much easier and much quicker than updating by hand. Changes aren't completely free of effort, though, so make sure that you will get extra value from an updated plan before spending the time and effort to develop one.

Internal changes/variances. Changes can result from project problems and variances as well as from requested or imposed changes by people outside the project team. Again, ordinary variances don't automatically require replanning and rebaselining. If you're a consistent week behind schedule, this is a bad thing, but the baseline will clearly show the variance and rebaselining will add no new information to help you solve your problem.

If, on the other hand, your project problems have gotten to a point where you have to rethink and replan to get from where you are now to some approximation of where you want to be, replanning may be the only technique that will achieve your goals. The old plan no longer measures effectively.

Circumstantial/environmental changes. Your plan always rests upon basic assumptions—the environmental conditions in which the work will take place. Like all assumptions, these carry certain elements of risk. If it happens that the project environment changes, the original plan and even the original destination may be overtaken by events. In that case, you have to rethink your project, and replanning is not optional.

When Not to Replan

Because replanning and rebaselining aren't free activities—they take time and effort you could spend elsewhere—our recommendation is not to do them lightly. If you're looking at ordinary variances and the basic direction is unchanged, the original baseline still points you in the right direction and gives you measurements you can meaningfully interpret. Spend your time and energy in higher producing activities.

Remember that the presence of a variance by itself is not proof you have a problem; it's simply a data point for you to analyze. And also remember that all the information you need to interpret a project probably isn't on the page in front of you. Your judgment, your understanding, and your insight into the entirety of the project is your most valuable tool.

Chapter 5:
Closing Your Project

PROJECT *CLOSEOUT* IS THE FINAL PHASE OF PROJECT management, in which you bring the project to a close, deliver the deliverables, ensure customer satisfaction, and do the administrative activities necessary to wind down the operation. It's also a great opportunity to get a head start on the next project by salvaging everything you might be able to reuse.

Closing Processes

The two formal processes in project closeout are known as *administrative closure* and *contract closeout*. Administrative closure involves the technical and operational tasks necessary to deliver project outputs and shut down the work. Contract closeout is an important step on any project that has used contracts, either by issuing contracts to others, or in many cases, performing the project as a contractor.

Depending on your organization's policies, contract closeout can involve numerous steps, including verification, completion of forms, negotiation of exceptions and change orders, final invoicing, and approval of invoices.

Not officially separate, but requiring a whole new world of attention, is the process of obtaining customer approvals, verifying deliverables, and ensuring overall satisfaction with the job. That can vary from being simple and straightforward to being a highly complex negotiation.

Typical Problems in Closing a Project

Problems in closing out a project fit into two overall categories: problems that arise in the process of closeout, and problems that have been ignored or missed in earlier stages of the project. Project closeout is everyone's final opportunity to ensure that we get what we want. Any needs unmet earlier are brought onto the table now.

There are other problems that tend to arise during closeout that are not necessarily leftovers from problems not previously resolved. These include:

Unexpected staff turnover. When projects near their ends, most of the technical work is done, and the pace of work tends to slow somewhat. At the same time, in most organizations, other projects are ramping up and need staff. The desire of your technical performers to seek new work and the need of other project managers for trained staff combine to make an irresistible force to raid your staff.

Missing documentation. The ability to do the work and the ability to keep good records of the work done aren't particularly compatible. Documentation is often thought of as a last-minute activity that can be done in a half-hearted way, and there's a scramble at the end of the project to get it done.

Completion of administrative deliverables. Your organization and your customer's organization normally have administrative requirements for projects, including processing of sign-offs and approvals, completion of forms and paperwork, and delivery of resource and dollar use information to appropriate managers. It's often the case that not all the mandatory administrative requirements are listed in a single place. Just when you think you're finally complete with the project, you discover an entire new set of activities!

Transition management. The transition from building something to using something, from designing something to manufacturing something, is fraught with challenges. From training to the inevitable small adjustments, from preparing documentation to overseeing the migration from old systems to new, this area requires careful planning and execution.

Rumors. On large multi-year projects, people begin to worry whether they'll have a home after the project is complete. Sometimes this worry is justified. If you know there will be some layoffs or terminations at the end of the project, you need to prepare for them. If, on the other hand, people will have continued employment, make sure they know about it, or else you'll have people jumping ship prematurely.

Customer Acceptance Issues

Customer acceptance would be fairly easy to achieve if customers never changed their minds. That, alas, is not the experience of most project managers.

In the stage of project Initiation, you did everything you could to understand fully the customer's needs and objectives, and that's the first part of managing customer acceptance. Throughout project Planning and project Execution, we recommended that you keep the customer in the loop, treating the customer as a member of the team. This has several advantages.

First, when the customer participates in the project, he or she naturally likes it better. Second, many times customer dissatisfaction is focused on relatively small details. You may not realize which details matter most, but when the customer is on the team, you get much better feedback. Third, when you are the technical expert and the customer merely has the need, you can legitimately shape customer expectations in the direction you think is appropriate.

When the project nears closeout, the customer may get nervous. Up until now, everything has had a certain tentativeness about it. Now, it's serious. When the customer accepts the project in its final form, the ability to seek changes is dramatically diminished. If the customer is unsure of his or her needs or wants, finalizing the project is a big decision. In that case, the success of the project may well depend on the quality of your relationship with the customer, and on whether you've earned the customer's confidence.

Prepare for final acceptance. Organize the initial documents, verify that all deliverables are present and correct, identify the measurements that show how you met the original objectives and approved changes, and deliver the product or output in a formal presentation or turnover. By giving the customer a tour of the results, you do a lot to build confidence and ensure finality.

The Administrative Close

Administrative closure is the process of verifying and documenting project results, formalizing acceptance of the product or service by the customer, collecting and reviewing project records, analyzing project effectiveness, and archiving information. The process can also entail reassignment or return of personnel and equipment. It's a necessary part of every project but sometimes not done well. The biggest reason it is deficient is because—well, let's face it—it's pretty boring. Few people enjoy the final wrap-up paperwork, and some otherwise successful projects have become hung up in the final details and ended badly.

As with most other stages in the project life cycle, begin thinking about closeout during the Planning phase. What will have to be done in order for the project to be considered completely finished? Who will do these various tasks? How long will it take? Prepare a Closeout Checklist to verify that everything has been properly completed. You can find numerous examples with a quick Internet search, though you'll always need to modify the checklist based on your unique needs.

Contract Closeout

The details of contract closeout vary by organization. Not only do you have to satisfy the administrative details of turnover and ensure customer satisfaction, but you must update all contract documentation to reflect final results, obtain necessary signatures, prepare and deliver invoices, and certify compliance with terms. Make sure you talk with your contracting and procurement professionals well in advance to ensure you do it right.

The Project File

The project file not only allows you to archive critical project information, but also helps you with the next step, which is analyzing the project for Lessons Learned. Some of this information needs to be part of the company's formal and legal archives, but other information may be stored more informally.

Check with your legal department on organizational policies about saving and discarding information, especially contractual information. Make sure you comply with all those policies. In general, saving project information is a good tool, because it provides you with an increasingly valuable base from which to develop estimates and risks for future projects.

Because full and proper archiving takes significant amounts of time and focus, it may be difficult to do it well. If you've maintained project files and a project binder throughout the process, archiving the project may simply involve a review of materials and moving them from the active part of your files to the storage portion.

Evaluate and Celebrate

At long last, our project has reached its conclusion. The deliverables are delivered, the customer is happy, and the paperwork is done. Time to move on? Almost, but not quite. There are two final elements that are part of a best practices approach to project management. These elements won't help the project that's just finished, but they put you on the path to better and better future project experiences. These steps are *project salvage and evaluation* (often known as "lessons learned") and *project celebration*, the final elements in project closeout.

Critical Questions for Project Evaluations

We strongly recommend that you make a formal project evaluation process a fundamental step in any project. There are enormous potential benefits to be gained from relatively minor effort. After all, every project, whether successful or not, demands substantial concentration and focus, creativity in problem solving, and a wide range of practical skills. Unfortunately, unless a specific effort is made to ensure the knowledge and experience earned on one project carries forward, much of the value is lost as the team turns to the next project.

It's important to distinguish a Lessons Learned program from its cousin "blamestorming" (the creative process of figuring out who will be the scapegoat for this project). In both activities, you do spend time figuring out what went wrong and how it happened.

In the second, once you've assigned guilt, the exercise is over. But in the first, the goal is not blame or faultfinding. For every mistake that was made by a specific individual on the team, there are usually several other people who could easily have made the same mistake. If all of us understand the mistake and know what to do in the future to avoid it, then we all make a profit.

Organize a Lessons Learned meeting and circulate a list of discussion questions as the agenda before the meeting. Here is a list of sample questions to start with:

- What did we do right?

- What things mattered most on this project?

- What things surprised us on this project that weren't in our plan?

- What things did we anticipate that turned out not to happen?

- Where could we improve?

- What mistakes did we successfully avoid making?

- What should we experiment with on our next project?

- What did we learn by doing this project?

- What could we automate or simplify that we do over and over again?

- What other value could we extract from the project we just completed?

- What skills did we need that we were missing on this project?

- What skills do we anticipate we need to improve our project performance?

- What value did we get from the formal planning or documentation?

- What value did we not get from the formal planning or documentation that we could strive for next time?

Documenting Lessons Learned

Look for all the different ways you can get evaluation information on your project. In addition to a formal Lessons Learned meeting, interview and survey your customers, your project sponsor, and others in and outside the organization who were affected by your project. Consider interviewing key vendors and contractors as well. Their specialized expertise and insight is an oft-neglected source of information.

Complete your project by developing a Lessons Learned document in the form of a report. To the extent that any part of the document is a discussion of project mistakes, avoid naming names. Even if your intent is not to cast blame, finding one's name in print associated with an error is not comforting to most people. Focus on the future. How will the next project or projects run better, more smoothly, with fewer errors, with higher quality, and with more accurate cost and schedule performance? Start this as an organizational tradition, and watch all the projects in the organization improve!

Setting Objective Goals for Project Improvement

Striving for project management maturity is an important goal in forward-thinking organizations, because successful projects are how the organization changes and grows for the future. It's normal for organizations to start without a formal project management process and stumble through a few projects before coming to the realization that planning and organization is critical to success.

Promoting project management as a policy

Successful organizational change always requires the participation of senior management, but it's not necessary that they be on board on Day 1. Often, one department or section in the organization starts seeing the value of formal project management methodology, and the result is more successful projects. As other departments and groups see that it works, they begin to adopt the methodology themselves. It's often best if a new management theory or policy proves itself operationally first, and then top management gets excited about it. Results matter more than theory, so start with the results and watch the theory take care of itself.

Get the organization on board. Distribute your Lessons Learned reports fairly widely so that others see the process and the outcomes, and you'll start your organization moving on the path to project management success. Offer to coach or assist other project managers on the skills you learn. As all of us who train have experienced, there's nothing like trying to teach someone else to stimulate your own learning.

Promote objective goals. Now that you have Lessons Learned from one project, what goals should you set for yourself and your team on your next project? The basic goals of meeting the Triple Constraint and having a happy customer at the end are always on the agenda, but what about some others?

Look for the parts of the process that have proven to be vulnerable. Is it common that your customers have trouble defining their actual requirements? Then a good goal might be to develop a questioning process to help customers pin themselves down appropriately. Have your estimates proven to be a little on the optimistic side? Decide why that's happening and work to reform the process of doing the work, or alternatively change your estimating methodology.

Establish benchmarks for quality improvement in project management based on current project performance. We can already do projects this well. How about moving the bar upward a little bit?

Celebrating the Victory...and the Team

Your success is ultimately given to you by the work and achievement of other people. It's appropriate for you as the project manager to accept some of the credit, because you would have had to accept all the blame. Honor and good policy demand, however, that you share that credit. Besides the demands of simple good behavior, there are a number of practical payoffs you receive when you celebrate the work and achievement of your team and of the individuals on your team.

If you ask people what they'd most like to have as a reward for outstanding performance, the overwhelming chorus is usually "money!" And money is certainly one way to reward good performance. But the project manager is often not the supervisor of all team members, and you may not have the opportunity or the power to give people financial rewards. You can recommend them for financial rewards if your organization provides them, and that's usually worth the effort, but money is frequently not an option.

Recognize that people often work more for self-esteem and self-actualization than for physical or material rewards. A sincere thank-you note (copies for the personnel file and for the supervisor of record or other appropriate senior managers) or some little tchotchke that provides a personal memento of the project experience has a surprisingly positive effect. The key is sincerity—if it's clear you mean it, people will like it. If they don't think you mean it, they'll take it but it won't improve performance particularly.

People can find enormous satisfaction in project work, because at its end you have something to show for your effort. The best kind of memorialization and celebration is something that reminds us of that effort and applauds our performance in achieving it. At the conclusion of building the Smithsonian National Air and Space Museum, all staff received a little certificate of thanks, each hand-signed by the director. Down at the bottom there was a tiny little souvenir: a one-inch square of silver fabric (complete with dry rot) taken from the restoration of Charles Lindbergh's *Spirit of St. Louis*. The cash value was insignificant, but the celebration and reminder of achievement was very real indeed.

Your souvenir may not be something with that kind of historical significance, but that's not what you need. Thoughtfulness, creativity, and a sense of shared achievement are what make tokens of recognition real and significant, and that's something within all our grasps.

About the Author

MICHAEL SINGER DOBSON, PMP, IS AN AUTHOR, consultant and popular seminar leader in project management, communications, and personal success, who brings a unique practical perspective to what works in the real world. He has trained people in well over 1,000 organizations on three continents on topics ranging from project management to career strategies. His down-to-earth style and practical advice comes from his management career positions, including Vice President of Discovery Software, Inc., Vice President/Marketing & Sales of Games Workshop, Inc., and Director of Marketing and Product Development for *Dungeons & Dragons®* creator TSR, Inc. He was a member of the research team that created and opened the Smithsonian National Air and Space Museum, the world's most popular museum.

He is a co-winner of the H. G. Wells Award for Miniatures Game Design and is a recipient of the Samaritan Medal for Peace and Humanitarian Services from the actual Samaritan people. He's also the world's only private owner of an Apollo spacesuit.

He lives in the suburbs of Washington, DC, with his wife and frequent co-author Deborah Dobson. They have one son, James, a graduate of West Point.

Selected Bibliography

Project Management Books

Successful Project Management (4ᵗʰ edition) (AMACOM Self-Study Sourcebook, 2015)

Creative Project Management with Ted Leemann (McGraw-Hill, 2010)

Managing Multiple Projects with Deborah Dobson (AMACOM Self-Study Sourcebook, 2011)

Practical Project Management: The Secrets of Managing Any Project On Time and On Budget (SkillPath Publications, 1996)

Project: Impossible — How the Great Leaders of History Identified, Solved, and Accomplished the Seemingly Impossible — and How You Can Too! (Lessons From History series*)* (Multi-Media Publications, 2013)

Project Management Essential Library: The Triple Constraints in Project Management (Management Concepts, 2004) — Translated into Chinese.

Project Management for the Technical Professional (Project Management Institute Press, 2001)

Project Risk and Cost Analysis with Deborah Dobson (AMACOM Self-Study Sourcebook, 2011)

Streetwise Project Management: How to Manage People, Processes, and Time to Achieve the Results You Need (Adams Media, 2003)

The Juggler's Guide to Managing Multiple Projects (Project Management Institute Press, 1999)

The Six Dimensions of Project Management with Heidi Feickert (Management Concepts, 2007)

Other Management Books

Enlightened Office Politics: Understanding, Coping With, and Winning the Game — Without Losing Your Soul with Deborah Singer Dobson (AMACOM, 2001)
Named one of the top business books of 2001 by *Library Journal.*

Managing Up: 59 Ways to Build a Career-Advancing Relationship With Your Boss with Deborah Singer Dobson (AMACOM, 2000)

Exploring Personality Styles: A Guide for Better Understanding Yourself and Your Colleagues (SkillPath, 1999)

Coping With Supervisory Nightmares: 12 Common Nightmares of Leadership and What You Can Do About Them with Deborah Singer Dobson (SkillPath, 1997) — also made into a video and audio.

Hiring and Firing with Paul Falcone (AMACOM Self-Study Sourcebook, mid 2012)

Training Skills for Team Leaders with Deborah Singer Dobson (SkillPath, 1998) — videotape and audio program.

Working With Difficult People (Second Edition) with William and Kathleen Lundin (AMACOM WorkSmart series, 2009)

Real-World Time Management (Second Edition) with Roy Alexander (AMACOM WorkSmart series, 2009)

Goal Setting (Second Edition) with Roy Alexander (AMACOM WorkSmart series, 2009)

Fiction

Fox on the Rhine (Forge, 2001) — Alternate selection of the Military Book Club and the Science Fiction Book Club; translated into Polish; was used as an answer on *Jeopardy!;* has its own Wikipedia page. (All novels co-authored with Douglas Niles)

Fox at the Front (sequel, Forge, 2003) – also with its own Wikipedia page.

MacArthur's War: A Novel of the Invasion of Japan (Forge, 2007) — Alternate selection of the Military Book Club and the Science Fiction Book Club

Other

AD&D® Battlesystem™ (game) (TSR, Inc., 1982)
   Won the H. G. Wells Award for Best Miniatures Game

Dragonlance Boardgame (TSR, Inc., 1983) — plus numerous other games and game supplements

H1 Bloodstone Pass (TSR, Inc., 1983) and sequels
   Featured on the television series *Stranger Things*

The Story of a Special Day (series, over 100 volumes completed to date) (Timespinner Press, 2014)

Watergate Considered as an Organization Chart of Semi-Precious Stones (Timespinner Press, 2013)

Improbable History (Timespinner Press, 2015), editor

How to Get Into a Military Service Academy (Rowman & Littlefield, 2015)

"Managing Instructional Design and Training Development and Delivery," (multiple authors) in *ISPI Handbook of Improving Performance in the Workplace, Volume I: Instructional Design and Training Delivery.* (Pfeiffer/Wiley, 2010)

"Decision-Making," (multiple authors) in *Applied Project Management for Space Systems (Space Technology Series)* (McGraw-Hill, 2008) and in modified form in *Applied Space Systems Engineering (Space Technology Series)* (McGraw-Hill, 2009)

"Ford Tri-Motor," "Lockheed F-104," "Fairchild FC-2," "Piper PA-12," in *Aircraft of the National Air and Space Museum* (Smithsonian Institution Press, 1976)